# Eerie Elegance Eats

## A Halloween Cookbook of Creepy Cuisine

by
Britta Peterson

BRITTA BLVD PUBLISHING

Eerie Elegance Eats is an original publication of Britta Blvd Publishing.

Britta Blvd Publishing
2532 Rose Way
Santa Clara, California 95051 USA
publishing@brittablvd.com

All text, photographs and illustrations copyright © 2017 by Britta M. Peterson
Published by arrangement with the author
ISBN: 978-0-9815871-3-4   0-9815871-3-5
www.EerieElegance.com

All rights reserved, which includes the right to reproduce this book or portions thereof in any form whatsoever except as provided by U.S. Copyright Law.
For information address Britta Blvd Publishing.

First edition: August 2017

Printed in the U.S.A.

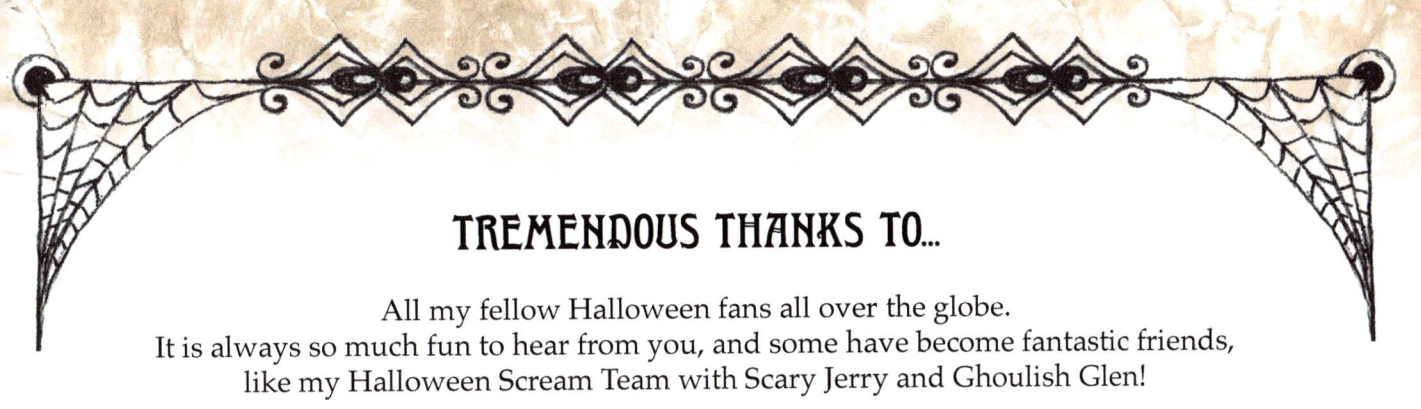

## TREMENDOUS THANKS TO...

All my fellow Halloween fans all over the globe.
It is always so much fun to hear from you, and some have become fantastic friends,
like my Halloween Scream Team with Scary Jerry and Ghoulish Glen!

My editing and development crew over the years: Glen, Jerry, Natasha, Nathania, Teje, Tracia, Robin, Ruth, Jules, and my mom Diane

My Creepy Cuisine Contest Winners who were so kind to give their permission to include their creations:
Teje, Dave & Wendy, Tracey, Ruth, Tracia, Lyle, & Glen

Kathy Henricks "Rosette Queen"
for her rosette recipe & tips from her years of experience

Angie Mathues for a marathon of frying five dozen Tasty Tarantulas!

All the "house-elves" who have helped me prepare party food over the past twenty years: Natasha, Melanie, Kael, Tracia, Doug B., Ashlyn, Kian, Shannon, Kathy, Diane, Lori, Sheila, Kevin, Nathania, Kaelyn, Angie, Ruth, Gail, Keith, Doug G., Christopher, Craig, Troy, Scary Jerry, and Ghoulish Glen!

All my party guests, friends & family over the years for being my captive audience, and inspiring me to show them new ideas every year!

I hope you enjoy
Eerie Elegance Eats!

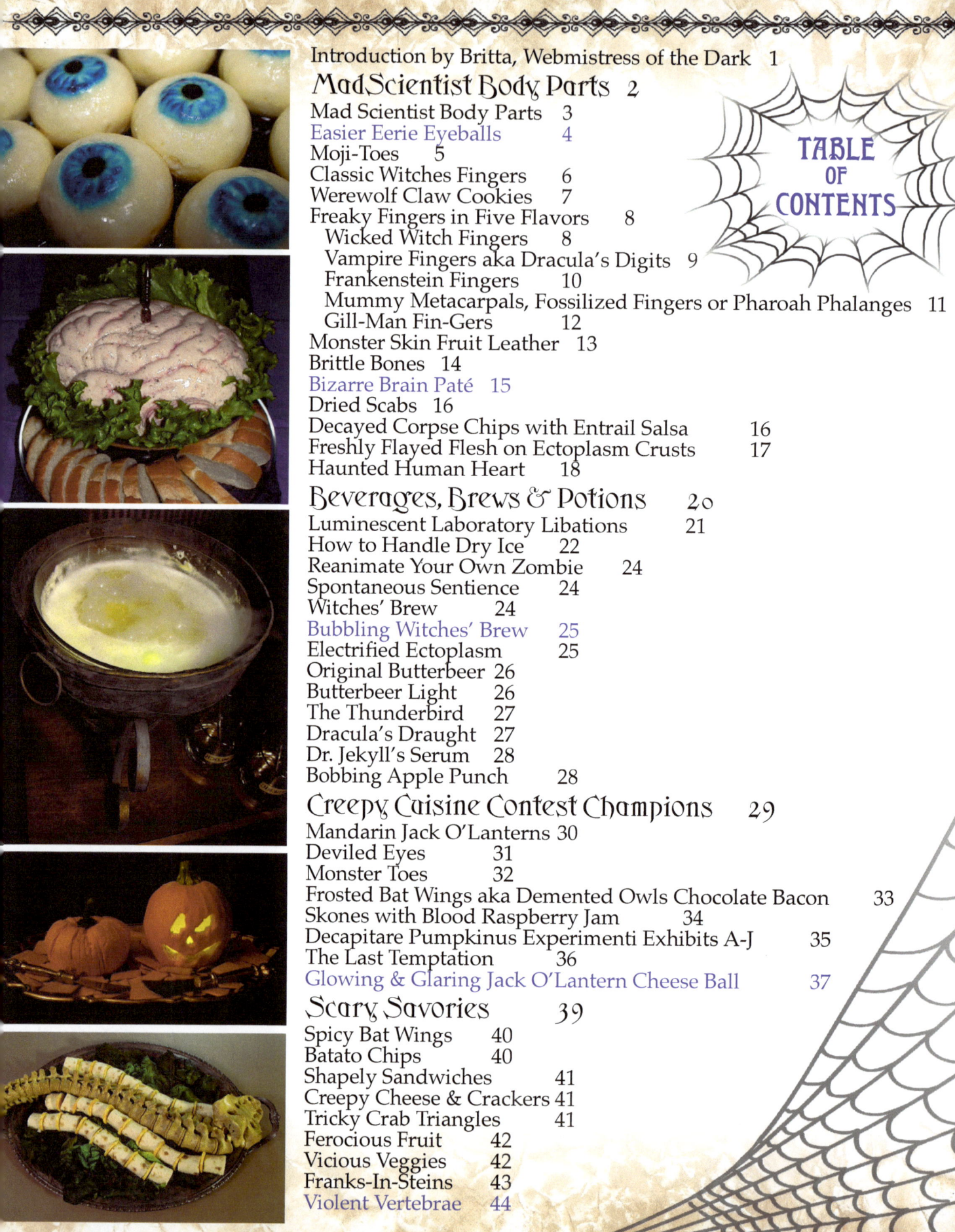

Introduction by Britta, Webmistress of the Dark  1

# MadScientist Body Parts  2

Mad Scientist Body Parts  3
Easier Eerie Eyeballs  4
Moji-Toes  5
Classic Witches Fingers  6
Werewolf Claw Cookies  7
Freaky Fingers in Five Flavors  8
   Wicked Witch Fingers  8
   Vampire Fingers aka Dracula's Digits  9
   Frankenstein Fingers  10
   Mummy Metacarpals, Fossilized Fingers or Pharoah Phalanges  11
   Gill-Man Fin-Gers  12
Monster Skin Fruit Leather  13
Brittle Bones  14
Bizarre Brain Paté  15
Dried Scabs  16
Decayed Corpse Chips with Entrail Salsa  16
Freshly Flayed Flesh on Ectoplasm Crusts  17
Haunted Human Heart  18

# Beverages, Brews & Potions  20

Luminescent Laboratory Libations  21
How to Handle Dry Ice  22
Reanimate Your Own Zombie  24
Spontaneous Sentience  24
Witches' Brew  24
Bubbling Witches' Brew  25
Electrified Ectoplasm  25
Original Butterbeer  26
Butterbeer Light  26
The Thunderbird  27
Dracula's Draught  27
Dr. Jekyll's Serum  28
Bobbing Apple Punch  28

# Creepy Cuisine Contest Champions  29

Mandarin Jack O'Lanterns  30
Deviled Eyes  31
Monster Toes  32
Frosted Bat Wings aka Demented Owls Chocolate Bacon  33
Skones with Blood Raspberry Jam  34
Decapitare Pumpkinus Experimenti Exhibits A-J  35
The Last Temptation  36
Glowing & Glaring Jack O'Lantern Cheese Ball  37

# Scary Savories  39

Spicy Bat Wings  40
Batato Chips  40
Shapely Sandwiches  41
Creepy Cheese & Crackers  41
Tricky Crab Triangles  41
Ferocious Fruit  42
Vicious Veggies  42
Franks-In-Steins  43
Violent Vertebrae  44

## Dastardly Desserts  45
Sneaky Slices with Golden Goo   46
Magical Mandrakes   46
Tooth Decay Fodder   47
Pumpkin Pasties   47
Donut Be Scared Peekaboo Pumpkins   48
Orange Pumpkin Icing   49
Foolproof Sugar Cookies   50
Buttercream Frosting   51
Royal Icing   51
Edible Medals   52
Ghoulish Gravestones   53
Tasty Tombstones   54

## Spooky Spiders & Skeletons   55
Startling Spiders   56
"Spiders of the Sea" Black Rice Crab Cakes   57
Slimy Spiders   58
Spiderweb Brie En Croute   59
Fried Spiders   59
Fal-Awful Arachnids Homemade Falafel   60
Tasty Tarantulas Spider Rosettes   62
The Gargantula Cheese Ball   64
Savory Spiders with Gooey Guts   66
Sourdough Spiders   67
Sourdough Bone Breadsticks   69
Crunchy Bone Breadsticks   70
Thin Bone Breadsticks   71
Sourdough Skeleton   72

## Dia de los Muertos Delights   73
Sinister Skulls Cream Cheese Calaveras   74
Chili Lime Corn Cups   75
Queso Fundido   76
Savory Skull Pizzas   77
Pequeño Pan de Muertos   78
Champurrado Chocolate   79
Creative Calavera Cookies   80
Dia de los S'Muertos   81

## Gingerbread Goodies   82
Ginger Web Cookies   83
Gingerbread Gargoyles   84
Ghoulish Gingerbread Haunted House   84

## Parting Words   97

## Eerie Elegance Eats Extras   98
Spooky Shopping   98
Gargoyle Guide   100
Creepy Cuisine Chef Cards   101

## About the Author   102

# INTRODUCTION BY BRITTA, WEBMISTRESS OF THE DARK

Welcome to Eerie Elegance Eats: A Halloween Cookbook of Creepy Cuisine! Not only are the costumes and decorations fun for Halloween, but I always have to see what creepy, ooky, or just plain icky party food I can make that is still tasty. Some friends may turn pale at the sight of my creations, but the brave ones discover that these dishes are quite delicious. I've been making the yummy gelatin Eerie Eyeballs since 1994, but some of my friends are often too squeamish to eat them!

My Halloween Recipes first went online in 1997, delightfully disturbing both children and grownups alike for over twenty years now. Many fans appreciate how my recipes are a niche between full-gore horror displays and cute but tame kid-friendly foods, making the world smile with a touch of spooky style. I am still thinking up new Creepy Cuisine to this day…a few recipes in this book haven't even been featured at my own parties yet!

Both my previous Eerie Elegance books have included some of my recipes along with Halloween party ideas and decor, but fans have requested all my recipes together in a single collection, so here are all the old favorites from both my previous books, including Creepy Cuisine Contest Winners, plus over THIRTY previously-unpublished new recipes!

Carry on creating the Creepy Cuisine within these pages, and feel free to add your own terrifyingly tasty touches when you feel inspired!

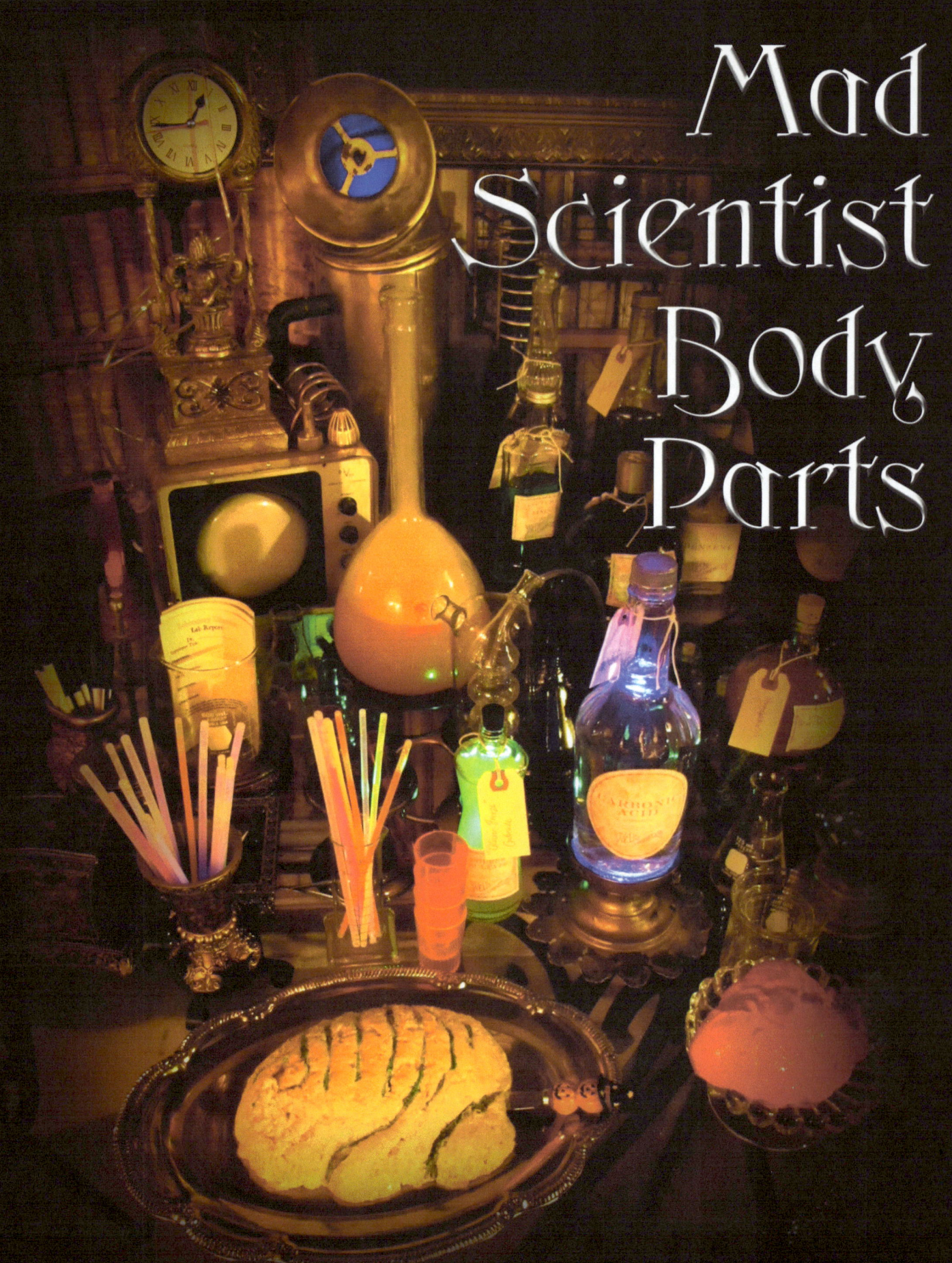

# MAD SCIENTIST BODY PARTS

My repertoire of recipes has acquired more and more body parts over the years, and since my "mad scientist" laboratory display has also expanded, I have arranged all the edible body parts together as a mad scientist experiment in process, complete with microscopes, notebooks, periodic tables, and lab coat hanging on the wall waiting for the doctor to return. Not only does this enhance the mad scientist theme nicely, but it also frees space on other tables for even more food, especially when guests bring their own devious dishes.

The Eerie Eyeballs, Bizarre Brain, Freaky Witches' Fingers and Haunted Human Heart have their own complete recipes listed separately. The bleeding hands are made in the same way as the Haunted Human Heart, using peach gelatin with evaporated milk as the flesh, with the same raspberry blood syrup in a plastic baggie bladder inside. The green substance in the large jar is an assortment of Gummy Body Parts purchased candies suspended in green "ectoplasm" soft-set lime gelatin. Deliciously disgusting!

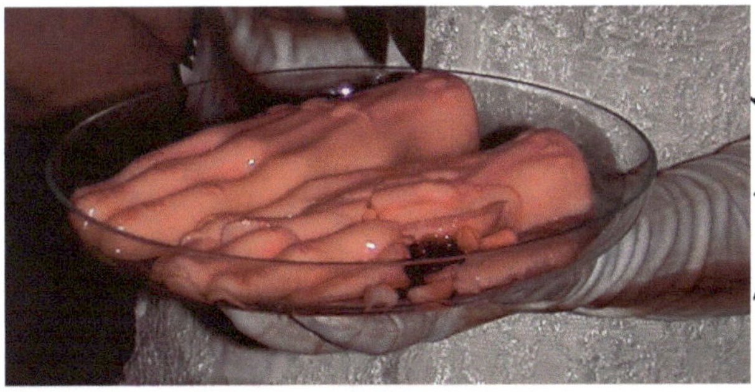

# EASIER EERIE EYEBALLS

I made my original Eerie Eyeball recipe the same way for years, and since I would multi-task stirring the eyeball goop melting the marshmallows and cream cheese while doing other party prep tasks, I never realized how long it really took until I filmed it. I was horrified and vowed that I would simplify the recipe! Here is an easier recipe that does not need a double-boiler or hand mixer and melts much more quickly, and also includes an easier painting technique.

**2 packets plain gelatin in 1 cup tepid water**
**8 oz (one brick) cream cheese (can be Neufchatel)**
**1 10 oz jar marshmallow creme (or 1 cup mini marshmallows)**
**1 cup cold pineapple juice**
**truffle candy molds or similar half-sphere molds**
**food coloring for irises (your choice of color)**
**black food coloring for pupils**
**piping tip or similar size lid for iris outline**
**solid small dowel, pen, or similar size flat round end for pupil**
**fine soft watercolor brush**

Bloom powedered gelatin first in the tepid water by letting it soak while you proceed. Put cream cheese into saucepan over medium heat and stir until smooth. Add marshmallows and stir until completely melted. Using marshmallow creme instead of mini marshmallows makes it melt even easier. After cream cheese and marshmallow mixture is smooth, stir in the bloomed gelatin until completely combined. Add the cold pineapple juice last, mixing again until smooth. The goop will be very runny, but after chilling it will set up into eyeball texture without being too chewy. Pour into molds and chill in fridge until set. You may still use the original melonballer technique to scoop eyeballs from a deep container after setting, but molds are much EASIER. This full recipe makes 9 dozen truffle-mold eyeballs, however this new recipe can be easily divided in half!

After eyeballs are set, gently unmold and arrange on the serving tray. Set out food coloring on a plate or tray. Use the watercolor brush to spread a good layer of iris color large enough for the back opening of the piping tip. Dip the back opening of the piping tip into the food coloring and twist. Aim center above one eyeball, gently lower onto the eyeball surface, and gently twist to apply consistent color in a full circle. Use the watercolor brush to gently brush lines from the circle inwards, leaving white space towards the center. Dip the back of the pen into black food coloring, making sure none will drip. Gently lower the pen into the center of the painted eyeball, twisting gently to transfer all the black in a clean circle for the pupil. If the eyeball surface isn't smooth, gaps may appear in the pupil, then you can touch up with the brush if you like. Refrigerate until you are ready to serve to your eyeball eaters.

# MOJI-TOES

I discovered drinking mojitos back in 2002, and since I keep growing mint in my garden, fresh mojitos are a staple for summertime parties with my friends. One Halloween guest was looking at the Mad Scientist Body Parts and started joking about "moji-toes" so of course I took on the challenge!

I first thought of an opaque gelatin shot since it would go with my other gelatin body parts, but the most difficult part was the toe shape. Even though I looked at ice cube trays and candy molds for a longer rounded end shape, I could not find any molds that looked enough like toes, so I made my own using polymer clay originals, washed them thoroughly, then made the molds with food-grade silicone putty now available at craft stores and online. I only made 9 toe molds, so I tailored my recipe to fit that much at once. By mixing up one batch at a time, you can keep enough Mojitoes safe in the fridge for several days until your party.

**Yields approximately 9 large monster toes.**

1 envelope plain powdered gelatin
1 1/2 c mojito mixer
1 oz (1/8 cup) light rum (optional)
1/2 c mini marshmallows

Pour 1 1/2 cups mojito mixer into a saucepan over medium low heat. Stir plain powdered gelatin into mojito mixer. After gelatin is dissolved, add 1/2 cup mini marshmallows and keep stirring until marshmallows are completely dissolved. Remove from heat and add 1 oz light rum if desired. Pour into well-oiled toe molds and refrigerate until set. Carefully remove the Moji-toes from the molds, accent the details with food coloring if you like, and serve.

### TRICKS & TIPS
I could not find any molds that looked enough like toes, so I made my own using polymer clay originals and food-grade silicone.

# CLASSIC WITCHES FINGERS

Over the years many people have developed their own recipes for edible fingers, but many puff instead of staying lean. I realized that the dough was very similar to a Christmas cookie recipe I had, so I just used neither baking powder nor baking soda and had a more shortbread-like recipe that keeps the detail perfectly, since it has no leavening. I now use my adapted recipe and it works every time.

**Yields 5 dozen**

**1 cup butter, softened
1 cup powdered sugar
1 egg
1 teaspoon almond extract
1 teaspoon vanilla
2 2/3 cups flour
1 teaspoon salt
3/4 cup almonds, whole, blanched or sliced
1 tube red decorator gel (optional, not pictured)**

In bowl, beat together butter, sugar, egg, almond extract and vanilla. Beat in flour and salt. Cover and refrigerate at least 30 minutes. Working with one quarter of the dough at a time and keeping remainder refrigerated, roll heaping teaspoonful of dough into finger shape for each cookie. Squeeze twice along finger length to create knuckle shapes. Press almond firmly into one end for nail. After arranging on the lightly greased baking sheets, make slashes with a paring knife across in several places to form knuckles. Clusters of three slashes for each knuckle looks best.

Bake in 325° F (160° C) oven for 20-25 minutes or until pale golden. Let cool for 3 minutes. Lift up almond, squeeze red decorator gel onto nail bed and press almond back in place, so gel oozes out from underneath. You can also make slashes in the finger and fill them with "blood." If you are opting for less gore, you will still need spare icing to glue the almond nails to the cookies after baking, since otherwise they fall off too easily during storage and serving.

When cool enough to stay intact, remove fingers from baking sheets and let cool on racks before storing. Repeat with remaining dough. Baked cookies will keep in an airtight container for at least two weeks. Unbaked mixed dough can be kept refrigerated for at least a week. Arrange for serving attractively on a plate, reaching up out of an urn of chocolate cookie crumb dirt, crawling out of a basket, or your own creative idea.

# WEREWOLF CLAW COOKIES

As my Scream Team was watching all the classic monster movies as research for our Haunted Hollywood Halloween party, we were inspired to widen our scope for my classic witches finger cookies. Why not other monsters, especially Werewolf Claw Cookies?

This cookie dough doesn't include nuts or nut flavors besides coconut, so omitting the cashew claws would be safe for nut allergies. Ironically these menacing cookies are vegan when using coconut oil and vegan egg replacer!

1 cup coconut oil, softened
1 cup powdered sugar
1 egg or equivalent vegan egg replacer
1 teaspoon vanilla extract
1 teaspoon salt
1 cup shredded sweetened flake coconut
1/8 cup special dark cocoa powder
1/4 cup water
2 2/3 cups all-purpose flour

for decoration:
1 cup shredded sweetened flake coconut in a plate or low bowl
whole cashews

In a mixing bowl, beat together coconut oil, powdered sugar, egg, vanilla, and salt. Beat in cocoa powder, then all-purpose flour, then after that is all mixed, add 1 cup shredded sweetened flake coconut. When using coconut oil do NOT chill this dough or it will become dry and too crumbly to form into shape. If you need to store the dough for a few days you can refrigerate it, but make sure you let it thaw all the way to room temperature before forming your claws.

Form a finger shape with the dough, then press firmly into shredded sweetened flake coconut so the coconut sticks into the dough. Sculpt the finger shape while pressing in the coconut flakes, then add a whole cashew as the claw in place on lightly greased cookie sheets, or use parchment paper or silicone mats. Bake at 325 degrees F (160 C) for 35 minutes or until the coconut flakes turn brown. If the cashew claws fall off after cooling, use a tiny dab of royal icing to glue them back in place.

Due to the coconut oil getting so crumbly when chilling, I do not recommend freezing these either before or after baking, but since they are cookies, they will keep fine in an airtight tin for two weeks or more, so you can make these Werewolf Claws well in advance for your Halloween party!

# FREAKY FINGERS IN FIVE FLAVORS

Freaky Witches' Fingers are an extremely popular twenty-year classic from my first book, but you can enhance your effects to turn the same basic recipe concept into a whole menagerie of monsters! Only bake these until the cookies are set, or browning could alter any colors you have added to the dough. The almond extract flavor goes well when using almond fingernails, but why not experiment with other flavors? My favorite flavor combinations are here, but feel free to substitute your own favorite extracts as you like. I do not recommend replacing the butter with coconut oil because the cookie shapes spread too much while baking instead of preserving the sculpted details, but vegan margarine and vegan egg replacer work fine.

## WICKED WITCH FINGERS

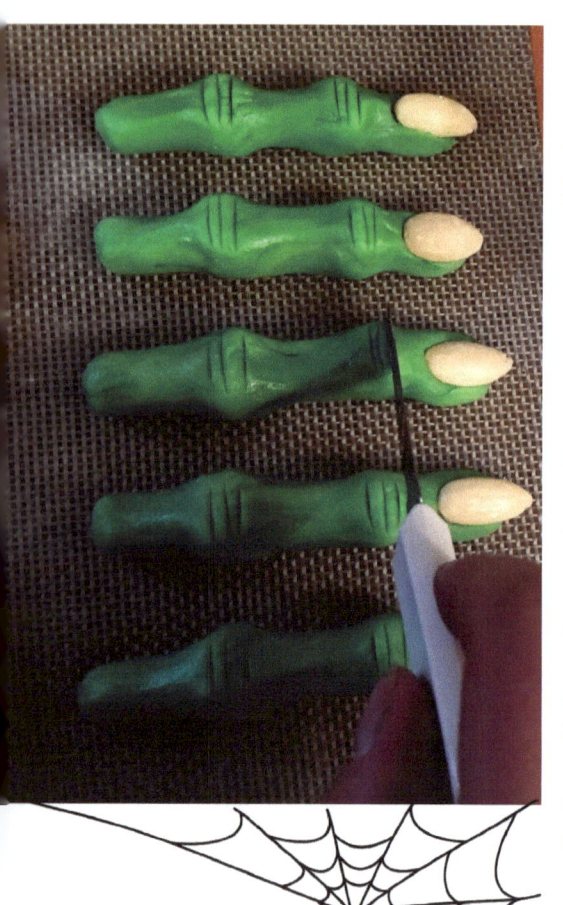

Adapt the original Freaky Witches' Fingers by using blanched whole almond fingernails plus green food coloring in the dough for Wicked Witch Fingers from a certain land over the rainbow.

**1 cup butter or vegan margarine, softened**
**1 cup powdered sugar**
**1 egg or equivalent vegan egg replacer**
**1 teaspoon almond extract**
**1 teaspoon vanilla extract**
**6 drops leaf green gel food coloring**
**1 teaspoon salt**
**2 2/3 cups all-purpose flour**
**whole blanched almonds**

Cream butter and sugar together. Add salt, egg, flavoring and food coloring, then mix until combined. Add the flour, then adjust the final color as necessary. Remember you can always add more color but you can't make it paler! Chill the dough at least one hour.

Form the Wicked Witch finger shapes by pressing the dough together to form knuckles. Place on a greased baking sheet close together since they will not spread while baking. Use a small knife to slash the knuckle wrinkles into the dough, then add the whole blanched almond fingernails.

Bake at 325F/160C for 30-35 minutes until set but not browned. Cool completely, then use royal icing to glue any loose fingernails on permanently. Store at room temperature in airtight baking tins for 2 weeks.

# VAMPIRE FINGERS AKA DRACULA'S DIGITS

Tint the dough an undead pale gray with pale fingernails, bloody red gel icing optional.

1 cup butter or vegan margarine, softened
1 cup powdered sugar
1 egg or equivalent vegan egg replacer
1 teaspoon vanilla extract
1 drop black gel food coloring
1 teaspoon salt
2 2/3 cups all-purpose flour
whole blanched almonds

Cream butter and sugar together. Add salt, egg, flavoring and food coloring, then mix until combined. Add the flour, then adjust the final color as necessary. Remember you can always add more color but you can't make it paler! Chill the dough at least one hour.

Form the vampire finger shapes by pressing the dough together to form knuckles. Place finished fingers on a greased baking sheet close together since they will not spread while baking. Use a small knife to slash the knuckle wrinkles into the dough, then add the whole blanched almonds as fingernails.

Bake at 325F/160C for 30-35 minutes until set but not browned. Cool completely, then use royal icing or blood red gel icing to glue any loose fingernails. Store at room temperature in airtight baking tins for 2 weeks.

# FRANKENSTEIN FINGERS

Use chocolate candies as blunt fingernails and tint the dough a reanimated greenish-gray. Either pick out the brown candies from the multicolor packages, or buy all-black chocolate shell candies online.

1 cup butter or vegan margarine, softened
1 cup powdered sugar
1 egg or equivalent vegan egg replacer
1 teaspoon peppermint extract
1 drop each leaf green & black gel food coloring
1 teaspoon salt
2 2/3 cups all-purpose flour
black or brown candy-shell chocolate candies, M&Ms or similar

Cream butter and sugar together. Add salt, egg, flavoring and food coloring, then mix until combined. Add the flour, then adjust the final color as necessary. Remember you can always add more color but you can't make it paler! Chill the dough at least one hour.

Form the oversized squared-off Frankenstein Finger shapes by pressing the dough together to form knuckles. Tuck extra chocolate candies in the bottom side of the finger dough. Place finished fingers on greased baking sheet close together since they will not spread while baking. Use a small knife to slash the knuckle wrinkles into the dough, then add the chocolate candies as stubby fingernails. Do not use chocolate chips since they will melt too much during baking.

Bake at 325F/160C for 30-35 minutes until set but not browned. Cool completely, then use royal icing to glue any loose fingernails on permanently. Store at room temperature in airtight baking tins for 2 weeks.

**TRICKS & TIPS**
Either pick out the brown candies from the multicolor packages, or buy all-black chocolate shell candies online.

# MUMMY METACARPALS FOSSILIZED FINGERS OR PHAROAH PHALANGES

Use powdered spices as centuries of decay on cookies sculpted like wrapped mummy fingers.

1 cup butter or vegan margarine, softened
1 cup powdered sugar
1 egg or equivalent vegan egg replacer
2 tablespoons ginger
2 tablespoons cinnamon
2 scant teaspoons allspice
2 scant teaspoons cloves
1 teaspoon salt
2 2/3 cups all-purpose flour

Mix the ginger, cinnamon, allspice and cloves together and reserve half the dry spice mixture for after baking. Cream butter and sugar together. Add salt, egg, and the other half of the mixed spices, then mix until combined. Add the flour until you have a consistent dough, then chill the dough at least one hour.

Form the mummy finger shapes by pressing the dough together to form knuckles. Use a small knife to cut the surface of the finger into strip shapes, and pry the edge so the edge stays up while baking. Place finished fingers on greased baking sheet close together since they will not spread while baking.

Bake at 325F/160C for 30-35 minutes until set but not browned. Cool completely, then mix the same ratios of powdered spices with vodka or water as thick paint and "antique" the cookies, especially getting the spice paint into the strip seams, then burnishing with the brush so the color blends over the cookie as centuries of dust and decay. Vodka evaporates more quickly than water so it does not soak into the cookie. Let dry, then store at room temperature in airtight baking tins for 2 weeks.

# GILL-MAN FIN-GERS

1 cup butter or vegan margarine, softened
1 cup powdered sugar
1 egg or equivalent vegan egg replacer
2 teaspoon lemon extract (turn it up to a-lemon!)
1 drop each leaf green, yellow & brown gel food coloring
1 teaspoon salt
2 2/3 cups all-purpose flour
1 cup chopped walnuts or almonds (optional)
whole almonds with skin on

Cream butter and sugar together. Add salt, egg, flavoring and food coloring, then mix until combined. Add the flour, then adjust the final color as necessary. Remember you can always add more color but you can't make it paler! Add chopped nuts last if speckles are desired. Chill the dough at least one hour.

Form the Gill-Man Fin-Ger shapes more rounded and pointed than human fingers. Use a small knife to cut the surface of the finger into large scale shapes, and pry and crimp each scale so the edge stays up while baking. Place finished fingers on greased baking sheet close together since they will not spread while baking. then add the whole almonds with skin as the claws, more pointing down than human fingernails.

Bake at 325F/160C for 30-35 minutes until set but not browned. Cool completely, then use royal icing to glue any loose fingernails on permanently. Store at room temperature in airtight baking tins for 2 weeks. If you'd like to add webbing between these Gill-Man Fin-Gers, you can make the Monster Skin Fruit Leather, cut to shape, and glue under the Fin-Gers with a little royal icing!

# MONSTER SKIN FRUIT LEATHER

Different creatures are different colors, so use your imagination when making your own Monster Skin Fruit Leather! I tried bright green kiwi fruit as Green Alien Skin and the webbing between the Gill-Man Fin-Gers, but you could use applesauce for Zombie Skin, blackberries cut out as Bat Wings, or strawberries or raspberries as Dried Jellied Blood...the possibilities are endless!

2 cups of ripe fruit chunks, pureéd
2 tsp lemon juice or 1/8 tsp ascorbic acid (optional to prevent darkening)
corn syrup or honey to taste, if needed

Pureé 2 cups of ripe fruit chunks, removing any large seeds, skins or stems. Add 2 tablespoons of lemon juice or ascorbic acid to prevent light-colored fruits from darkening. If the puree is too tart, add corn syrup or honey to taste, since using table sugar will crystallize over time. Applesauce can be dried alone or added to any fresh fruit pureé as an extender. It decreases tartness and makes the leather smoother and more pliable. You can even use frozen fruit but thaw it before pureéing. You can also experiment with adding powdered spices or flavor extracts, but start with only 1/8 tsp for 2 cups of fruit puree to taste.

Line a 13"x15" edged cookie sheet with plastic wrap, being careful to smooth out wrinkles. The low oven temperature will not melt the plastic wrap. Do not use waxed paper or foil. Pour the fruit pureé mixture into the prepared pan and spread evenly to about 1/8" thick, but avoid the edges or the plastic wrap might fold over onto your fruit spread. Dry fruit leather in your home oven at 170 degrees Fahrenheit no longer than 4 hours, until no indentation appears when touching the center of the leather. Once it is cool, roll up using the same plastic, and store up to 1 month at room temperature, or up to 1 year tightly rolled in the freezer. When ready to serve, cut shapes with a knife or cookie cutters as desired, pull away the excess leather, then trim the plastic wrap so each shape can be served individually.

You can use a food dehydrator if you have one, with much less risk of browning in low oven heat. If you have sunny dry weather, instead of using your oven, you can try the old-fashioned way of drying your fruit leather outside under a cheesecloth tent to protect from critters and falling leaves, but it might take up to 2 days of full sunshine. I remember my parents drying fruit leather in our yard in hot central California when I was little!

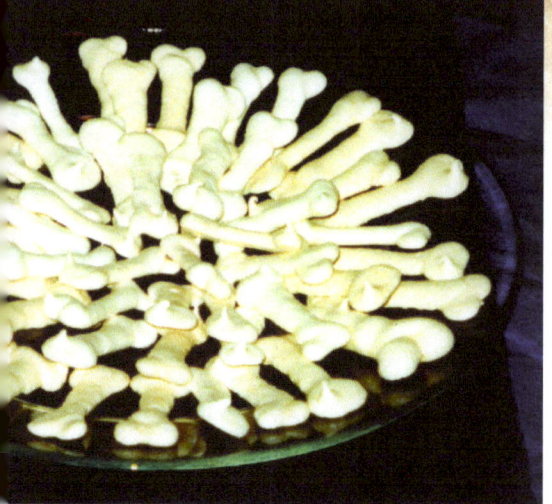

# BRITTLE BONES

Bone cookies are also not unusual, but I wanted a crispy bonelike texture for my cookies, so meringue's the thing and naturally bakes to a nice bone color without additional decorating. These are fragile, so some will break when removing them from the parchment paper, and they absorb moisture in the air and get gooey, so bring these out only immediately before guests arrive and don't set them near a fog machine, punch bowl or other sources of moisture if possible.

**Yields approximately 14 dozen small finger bones**

3 large egg whites
1/4 tsp cream of tartar
1/8 tsp salt
2/3 cup white sugar
1/2 tsp vanilla

Preheat oven to 200º F. Line cookie sheet with brown paper bag or parchment. In a medium sized bowl at high speed, beat egg whites, cream of tartar and salt till fluffy. Gradually beat in sugar. Add vanilla. Place in pastry bag fitted with a medium plain piping tip. Pipe 3" bone shapes onto parchment or brown paper bag. Bake 1 hour until set. Turn off oven, dry in oven 1 hour. Be sure to store in completely airtight reusable plastic food containers or they will become soggy from moisture in the air.

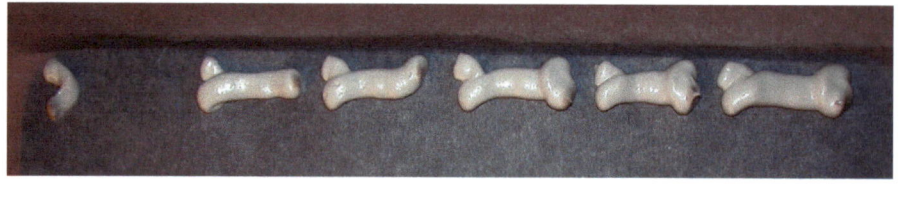

# BIZARRE BRAIN PATÉ

One year in July a friend gave me a brain mold for my birthday, obviously knowing my love of Halloween, so I used a recipe I had found for Mardi Gras and adapted it for my brain mold. You could use a sweet gelatin recipe like other body parts, but I thought menu balance with a savory addition was a better choice. The shrimp gives a nice pale pink smooth brain texture, and I use a fine watercolor paintbrush with some watery gray food coloring to accent and shade the brain folds. The leftovers make great sandwiches!

**half a can cream of mushroom soup (full can is 10 3/4 oz)**
**4 ounces cream cheese, softened (can be lowfat Neufchatel)**
**1 (1/4 oz) envelope powdered unflavored gelatin, softened in 1/4 cup water**
**1 pound frozen cooked shrimp or crab meat, finely chopped**
**1/2 cup mayonnaise**
**1 Tbsp lemon juice**
**Tabasco or creole seasoning to taste**

Pour the powdered unflavored gelatin into 1/4 cup water and let stand to bloom. Chop the frozen shrimp finely in a food processor or blender, until almost a paste. This is easier when the shrimp is still frozen hard. Heat undiluted soup and mix in the half-block of cream cheese. Remove the mushrooms or blend the soup before adding to the mixture if you are concerned they will show in your brain texture. Stir in softened gelatin and blend well. Fold in remaining ingredients and pour into a lightly-oiled mold. Chill until firm and serve with your favorite crackers.

### TRICKS & TIPS
You could use a sweet gelatin recipe like other body parts, but I thought menu balance with a savory addition was a better choice.

# DRIED SCABS

Yes, another nasty name for an otherwise mediocre dried fruit, but call them "scabs" and all of a sudden no one will eat them!

Arrange the dried cranberries in a bowl or dish. Be sure you have a sign to identify them as something spooky. You can use any small flat dried fruit like currants, cherries, or even blueberries, but raisins are usually too plump to be scabs.

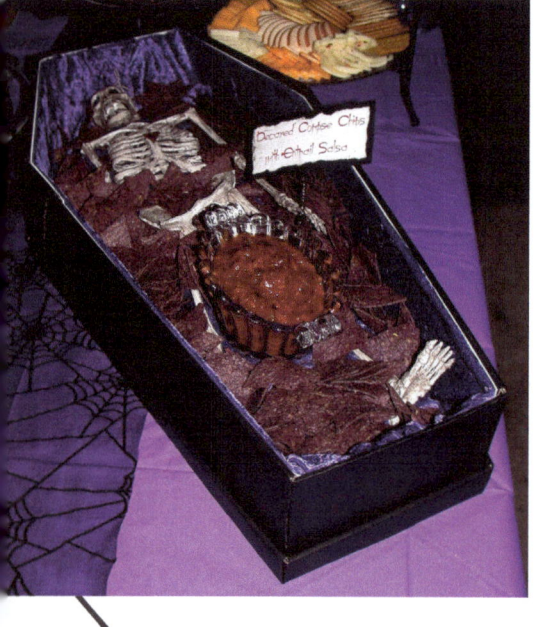

# DECAYED CORPSE CHIPS WITH ENTRAIL SALSA

As you can tell, often a very normal dish can be turned nasty just by giving it a disgustingly clever name. Think up your own names for your favorite appetizers to give them a Halloween spin.

**blue corn tortilla chips**
**coffin**
**salsa**

This isn't so much a recipe as it is a creative display. Arrange the blue corn chips in a napkin-lined coffin in the shape of a long-dead corpse. The natural blue corn chips have almost a dusky shade of brown in them that hints of decayed skin. Serve with a nice blood-red chunky salsa as accompanying entrails.

When I found a larger coffin that happened to fit a rubber skeleton I had for years, I lined the coffin with crushed velvet, propped up the skeleton inside so he wasn't completely buried in chips, arranged the chips around him, and set the crystal bowl of "entrails" between his calves. If you cannot find a coffin, find a clean plastic skull or assorted bones, put them in a large serving bowl, then arrange the blue chips around the bones as the decaying flesh.

# FRESHLY FLAYED FLESH ON ECTOPLASM CRUSTS

I was looking for more savory options for my maniacal menu, so I remembered the ever-popular smoked salmon with cream cheese and came up with these. Be sure to use the vivid pink oil-packed smoked salmon to really look like freshly flayed flesh!

**Yields about 3 dozen bite-sized appetizers**

1 package oil-packed sliced smoked salmon
1 package cream cheese (can be lowfat Neufchatel)
1 package crackers, melba toasts, bagel chips, or be creative!

Cut the smoked salmon into small thin strips. Spread a dollop of cream cheese on each cracker, then place a strip of smoked salmon curled on top of the cream cheese. This is another standard tasty appetizer just renamed to be gory for the season!

### TRICKS & TIPS
Be sure to use the vivid pink oil-packed smoked salmon to really look like freshly flayed flesh!

# HAUNTED HUMAN HEART

It probably surprises no one that I have been a fan of Penn & Teller's brand of dark humor for years, so I had not only seen them in person including getting autographs, but also read their book "How to Play With Your Food" (© 1992 by Buggs & Rudy Discount Corp.), so had seen their Bleeding Heart recipe and wanted to try it someday. I finally had my chance when I found a plastic human heart mold more than a decade ago at a specialty gift store around Halloween season. The mold came with a very similar recipe to make the gelatin opaque, but not any instructions to make it bleed, so I adapted Penn & Teller's recipe to create my own, and it has been one of my Halloween favorites ever since. You can find human heart molds online as well as at local Halloween stores. Penn & Teller used a Valentine's Day-style heart-shaped cake pan, but for Halloween I think using the human heart mold improves on their concept one-hundred percent!

I display my heart onto a crystal pedestal plate, then use food coloring and a small brush to accent the veins. I even use red food coloring to shade the muscle contours, since it really does make a difference. One year I had a cardiology intern attend my party, and she said my gelatin heart looked very realistic. Needless to say I was very proud at such high praise! I use my large Psycho-style butcher knife to sever and serve my Haunted Human Heart.

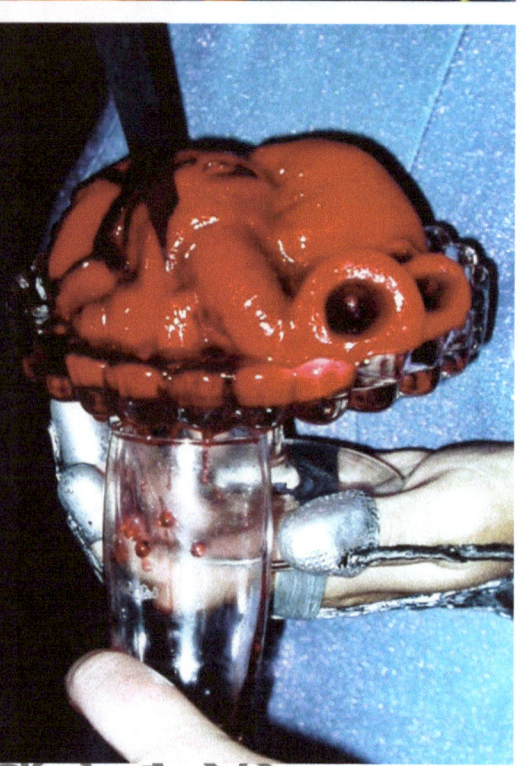

**For the heart:**
1 large 6 oz box raspberry gelatin dessert
small 5 oz can of unsweetened evaporated milk (can use fat-free)
1 packet unflavored powdered gelatin
1 cup boiling water

**For the blood:**
1/2 cup light corn syrup
1/2 cup raspberry syrup drink flavoring
1 Tbsp raspberry liqueur (optional)
1 drop blue food coloring
1 thin plastic non-zip sandwich bag

Thoroughly wash your mold, especially all the detail where the veins are. When completely dry, spray the mold with non-stick cooking spray. Use a larger bowl or crumpled foil around the outside to support your mold so the top surface will be level. Put the flavored gelatin in a large bowl and stir in 1 cup of boiling water. Stir about 3 minutes until completely dissolved. When slightly cooled, stir in the evaporated milk for one minute, otherwise the milk might curdle. Pour half of the mixture into the heart mold and refrigerate until it is soft-set, as the box instructions recommend for adding fresh fruit.

While the mold is setting, mix the corn syrup and raspberry syrup, plus raspberry liqueur if you like, with one drop of blue food coloring for a nice deep red blood color. Pour your blood into one corner of the thin plastic bag, squeeze the bag carefully to prevent air bubbles, then tie a knot so that the bladder will fit completely inside the rest of the mold, with enough space so gelatin will completely surround the bag. Trim the extra plastic off at the knot. Once the gelatin is soft-set and will support the bag of blood but without a skin on top of the gelatin, arrange the bag of blood, pour the remaining gelatin mixture up to the top of the mold, then refrigerate overnight. If you wait too long to add the remaining gelatin, the layers will not meld together, then your illusion is ruined when the top slides off the bottom, revealing your secret bag of blood!

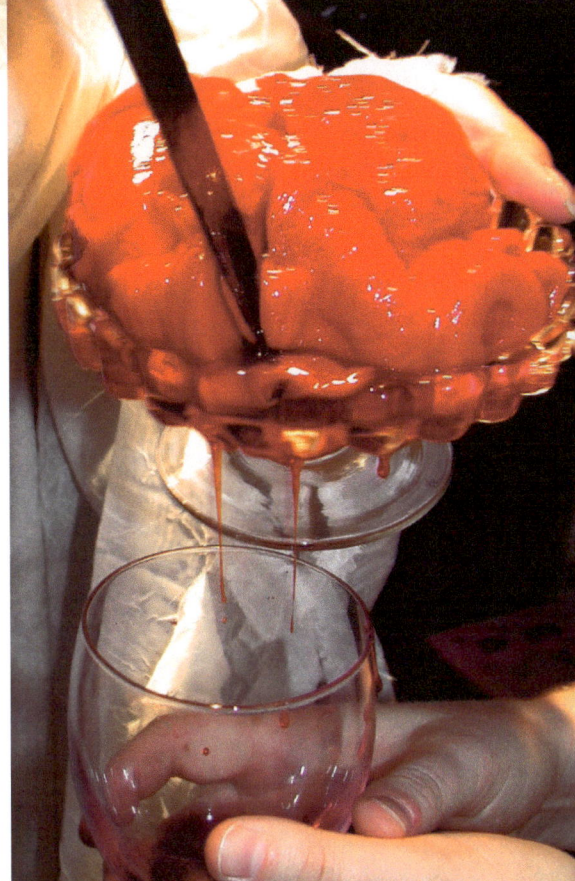

Once the gelatin is completely set, gently remove the heart from the mold and place on a serving plate, then use food coloring and a small soft watercolor brush to accent the veins. Use red food coloring to shade the contours of the muscle tissue, and blue food coloring to accent the veins. As you can see in the photo above, an unpainted heart is still alarming, but the accents make it so much more realistic. Refrigerate until the party, then display proudly, clarifying to all your guests that "Yes, that is our dessert!"

When ready to sever and serve, call all your guests to come watch the Haunted Human Heart. Enlist a volunteer to hold a glass or bowl to catch the spilling blood. Using a large knife, the scarier the better, stab directly down into the heart, making sure you poke the point of the knife into the plastic bag of blood. Twist the knife to widen the hole in the bag, then guide the knife down to cut a slice through the edge of the heart. Widen the opening in the heart so blood begins to flow. Gently tilt the plate so the blood can easily flow into the cup in your volunteer's hand as your guests all groan in disgust. If anyone actually wants to eat a slice, be careful not to serve any chunks of the plastic bag, and be sure to drizzle extra blood on each slice. If you have willing bodies, feel lucky, since I often have no one willing to eat any of my heart except me!

### TRICKS & TIPS
Use a large Psycho-style butcher knife to sever and serve your Haunted Human Heart.

# Beverages, Brews & Potions

# LUMINESCENT LABORATORY LIBATIONS

Ever since I turned my lab display into a mix your own experiment activity, I have been looking for ways to make edible liquids glow safely. There are references online that spinach juice or milk will glow under ultraviolet light, but I have tested them and they haven't worked for me. The only ones that are reliable are tonic water with quinine that glows blue, even diet tonic as long as it has real quinine, and vitamin B-12 glows green. Some sports drinks have B-12 in them, but not enough to glow, so I have crushed B-12 vitamin pills into dust and added one pill to 2 quarts of water. That glows a nice green, but it tastes absolutely horrible! Mixing tonic and B-12 together gives a beautiful glowing aqua teal color as shown here, but since I don't like tonic either, I can't even drink it. A little black vodka on top gives some nice shading.

I have given up on the edible iridescence and moved onward to using colored lights under the bottles and in bowls of ice cubes. This works quite well, but requires some crafting and some investment in the lights. For the lighted bases you can use any colored tealights, even color-changing lights, but if you want to use the lights in the same container as ice cubes, invest in submersible floral lights shown here that are safe to use completely submerged in water. I have found them online for about $3 each plus shipping, and they are great. They are slightly smaller than normal tealight size, they twist on and off instead of a switch, and the batteries last a long time. I tried them first with purple, and they give off enough ultraviolet spectrum to make the fluorescent items glow, so then I bought an assortment of colors, including a few color-changing lights. The color-changing lights are really fun, but I like having others stay one color so there is variety in the laboratory. You can also buy lighted ice cubes, but you cannot change the batteries in those since they are permanently sealed.

# HOW TO HANDLE DRY ICE

Dry ice creates a wonderful and fairly cheap smoke effect, but there are safety concerns. Any reputable dry ice supplier should give you a safety pamphlet when selling you their dry ice, so pay attention to those instructions as well as these tips.

"Dry ice" is solid carbon dioxide ($CO_2$), which is the majority of what animals, including humans, exhale every time they breathe, so the carbon dioxide molecule itself is not toxic. The bubbles in any carbonated drink like your favorite soda are mostly carbon dioxide bubbles. However, to force carbon dioxide into solid form, it requires a much lower temperature than ice made from water. This means that the severe cold of dry ice can cause burns to unprotected skin, so please be EXTREMELY careful when handling dry ice and using it around food or beverages. The fun part about solid carbon dioxide is that at standard room temperatures and above, it skips the usual "melting" transition from solid to liquid before turning into vapor, so it goes directly from solid to vapor, called "sublimation," which is the fog or "smoke" you see. The warmer the temperature around the dry ice, the quicker the sublimation process, which is why warm water is often recommended to get the rolling bubbles you see so often in mad scientist displays or witches' cauldrons.

When dry ice is put into warm water, the sublimation process continues until the water is cooled below the sublimation point, which means solid water ice forms as a crust around the dry ice. Even adding more warm water to the container at this point does not trigger sublimation again until the crust of water ice is removed. The best technique around this problem is to use the smallest chunks of dry ice that you can (even little chips work for a minute or two), since then the dry ice all sublimates away before the water is cooled too much. This also requires more "babysitting" your display since the smaller chunks disappear into vapor more quickly as well. Remember - you do NOT want anyone to eat or even touch any solid dry ice with any bare skin, let alone fingers, tongues or lips, since it can harm them. Then how have I used it in my punch cauldron safely? Well, I use a large 12-quart cauldron for my witches' brew, which is quite deep. Dry ice is heaviest so it will sit on the bottom, and my ladle doesn't reach all the way to the bottom of the cauldron without a lot of effort, so I was not that concerned. If you have carbonated soda in your punch, it's really cool when you get really big bubbles filled with the fog that pop at the surface, releasing a puff of "smoke" into the air.

I finally found a safe, reliable solution for putting dry ice into any size cauldron. A tea infuser ball is too small, since you would be refilling it every minute or so, however a large spice ball for mulled cider or wine has enough small holes to allow the fog to escape but not any physical chunks of dry ice. This is definitely worth the $8 I spent compared to my various prototypes made from hinging strainers together. Filling the spice ball with small chunks of dry ice lasted a good 15-20 minutes of vigorous bubbling, which is about as much time you get when dumping a bowlful of chunks directly into the cauldron. It comes with a chain to hang on the edge of the pot for easy retrieval, but in a punch bowl cauldron, you can always use the punch ladle instead if the chain falls in accidentally. I intend to use my spice ball for all cauldron dry ice effects from now on.

Many party stores will have seasonal Halloween sales of dry ice, but they usually charge more than if you look up "dry ice" in your local yellow pages. Some larger grocery store chains are now carrying a small bin of dry ice near the normal party ice bags. Bring an airtight ice chest with you to carry your dry ice home and help keep it as cold as possible until you want to use it. Do NOT put dry ice in your home freezer since the freezer can be permanently damaged! Try not to get your dry ice until the day of your party, or at least no earlier than the evening before your party if necessary. 50 pounds is usually enough to last through my party for my 12-quart cauldron of witches brew, my tabletop mad scientist display and a few other displays, plus some leftover the next day for my photo shoot of my decorations. I use a little hammer and an icepick on my wooden cutting board to smash smaller chunks from the large slabs, then use a plastic or freezer-safe ceramic bowl with thick gloves to scoop some chunks into the bowl then carry it to whatever liquid I'm using. By using the small chunks and leaving the rest in larger chunks together inside the ice chest still wrapped in their original paper wrappers, they help keep each other cold enough to last longer. You will need to keep adding more chunks of dry ice to your cauldron every 20-30 minutes or so to keep it bubbling really strongly, but gentler wisps of fog will keep going for longer. This "bubble maintenance" job to keep all the dry ice displays going while guests are still arriving is a good one to give to someone else while you continue preparing party food or are putting on your own costume. Once most guests have settled in, no longer paying as much attention to the cauldron, "bubble maintenance" can take a break, returning later if you like.

After all these warnings please still be aware that you need to use your own judgment about using dry ice around food and especially in beverages. If your party is for kids or teenagers, I would not put any dry ice in the actual punch at all, even inside a spice ball, nor would I if it was a rambunctious party with alcohol flowing so much people might not remember that solid dry ice can burn them. If your guests are reasonable adults and generally behave themselves, you might decide you can safely use dry ice in your witches' brew, too. Err on the side of caution if you are not sure of your guests. You know how your own party guests will behave better than I could ever guess.

# REANIMATE YOUR OWN ZOMBIE

This is a mad scientist experiment individual serving alcoholic cocktail in a small glass.

**hydrochloric acid = light rum**
**perchloric acid = spiced rum**
**tincture of iodine = dark rum**
**sulfuric acid = Bacardi 151**
**citric acid = pineapple juice**

"To Reanimate Zombies: Into a small beaker, pour equal parts hydrochloric acid, perchloric acid, tincture of iodine & sulfuric acid. Add a splash of citric acid, stir and feed to your corpse for instant reanimation."

# SPONTANEOUS SENTIENCE

This is a mad scientist experiment individual serving alcoholic cocktail in a small glass.

**benzene = peach schnapps**
**lactic acid compound = caramel cream liqueur**
**(can substitute Irish cream liqueur or similar)**
**life blood extract = raspberry syrup**

"Spontaneous Sentience: Pour benzene into a small beaker. Slowly add lactic acid compound as your brain tissue appears, then carefully add the life blood extract to the brain tissue."

# WITCHES' BREW

This recipe fills a 12-quart cauldron.

**four 48 oz cans pineapple juice**
**one 96 oz bottle orange juice**
**four 2 liter bottles lemon-lime soda**
**one 1.75 liter bottle vodka**
**one 1.75 liter bottle rum**

All measurements are approximate. Adjust to your own taste and mix well. Pour into your cauldron with chunks of dry ice to create the bubbling steam effect. For safe dry ice, fill a large spice ball with small chunks of dry ice and place into the brew. Do NOT to drink or eat any chunks of dry ice - you can get burned by the extreme cold!

# BUBBLING WITCHES' BREW

I have made several witches' brews throughout my Halloween history, but this one is my new favorite because of the snot-like brownish-green color and the huge foamy scum bubbles filled with fog that pop open with smoke escaping from the surface. From its disgusting appearance you'd never know it's just delicious lime sherbet, pineapple juice and ginger ale!

**green lime sherbet**
**2 quarts pineapple juice**
**2 liters ginger ale**

Place a few scoops of lime sherbet into the cauldron or punch bowl. Pour in the pineapple juice and ginger ale in equal parts until the container is full. For safe dry ice, fill a large spice ball with small chunks of dry ice and place into the brew. The carbonation in the ginger ale turns the sherbet into scummy foam, the pineapple juice makes the brew opaque to hide the spice ball, and the foamy bubbles fill with dry ice fog that eventually pop, leaving wisps of smoke rising from the surface of your Bubbling Witches' Brew!

# ELECTRIFIED ECTOPLASM

This is one of my suggested experiments in the Library Laboratory. I made a special version for myself in my skull goblet, using a small tea infuser ball with a small chunk of dry ice inside, and I was extremely careful not to touch skin to the tea ball or the dry ice! The serving jar of Ectoplasm is lighted from below using the Luminescent Laboratory Libations technique, and green lime gelatin dessert glows very nicely!

**Ectoplasm = green lime gelatin dessert, made according to instructions and scooped in chunks into a serving jar**

**Citric Acid = pineapple juice in a laboratory bottle**

**Tincture of Zinc = green melon liqueur in a laboratory bottle**

**Aqua Fortis = vodka in a laboratory bottle**

"To Electrify Ectoplasm: Scoop ectoplasm into a beaker. Add citric acid, aqua fortis, and tincture of zinc. Stir gently so as not to disturb the ectoplasmic structure and release the spirits too soon. Different proportions will give you varying levels of spirits released."

# ORIGINAL BUTTERBEER

This Butterbeer recipe was originally created for a wizard party, now appearing annually for Halloween by popular demand!

**Makes 2 quarts.**

**1 cup butterscotch schnapps
7 cups cream soda (almost one 2 liter bottle)**

Carefully mix just before serving, adding the schnapps to the soda then stirring gently to mix well, or the fizz will dissipate too soon. To keep butterbeer on hand, pour 1 cup cream soda out of the 2-liter bottle, quickly add 1 cup butterscotch schnapps, and recap the bottle. There is not much alcohol content in the butterbeer mixture, just enough to make a small elf tipsy and to give it the warm, buttery aftertaste to the fizzy cream soda.

**TRICKS & TIPS**
Mix & match the Butterbeer ingredients in any combinations you like!

# BUTTERBEER LIGHT

I improved on the well-loved Original Butterbeer recipe -- now all the alcohol and calories have been charmed away!

**Makes 2 quarts.**

**1 cup sugar-free butterscotch
or English Toffee flavoring syrup
7 cups diet cream soda (almost one 2 liter bottle)**

Carefully mix just before serving, adding the butterscotch flavoring to the soda then stirring gently to mix well, or the fizz will dissipate too soon. To keep butterbeer on hand, pour 1 cup cream soda out of the 2-liter bottle, quickly add 1 cup butterscotch flavoring, and recap the bottle. Completely sugar-free and alcohol-free!

# THE THUNDERBIRD

The shimmery liqueur in this recipe has edible silver dust in solution so it can make any cocktail look magical, perfect for your wizard potions laboratory!

In the wizarding world, the Thunderbird is a large, avian creature native to North America which possess multiple and powerful wings known to change colors as they summons storms, with iridescent feathers shifting from various shades of gold, to electrifying blue, to grey and silver, to white, and even to deep navy. A close relative of the Phoenix, the Thunderbird can create storms as it flies and is highly sensitive to danger.

**The Thunderbird**

**1 part ginger ale**
**1 part chai tea syrup**
**1 part blackstrap rum**
**1 part Viniq shimmery liqueur**

Pour equal parts ginger ale, chai tea syrup, and blackstrap rum over ice, then top with Viniq shimmery liqueur. Watch the swirling storm clouds brewing in your glass, sparkling with the magical powers of the Thunderbird!

# DRACULA'S DRAUGHT

**3 parts cranberry-raspberry juice**
**1 part raspberry syrup**
**1 part pineapple juice**
**2 parts lemon-lime soda**
**1 part vodka (optional)**

This cocktail can be mixed individually or mixed in larger quantities as a punch, preferably in a clear bowl, glass cauldron, or skull fountain cauldron so everyone can appreciate the opaque blood-red color. This recipe is easily adapted for all ages by leaving the alcohol on the side for adults to spike their own glasses as they wish.

# DR. JEKYLL'S SERUM

**2 parts blue energy drink**
**1 part tonic water (can be diet tonic water)**
**1 part citrus vodka (optional)**

This cocktail is not only vivid blue in normal light, but it will glow a bright blue under ultraviolet "black" light! This drink is easily adapted for all ages by leaving the alcohol on the side for adults to spike their own glasses as they wish. Mix individual cocktails or prepare larger quantities in advance in a pitcher for easy pouring. Serve in test tubes in your laboratory but be careful about unleashing your Mr. Hyde dark side!

# BOBBING APPLE PUNCH

Bobbing for apples has been a Halloween party game for over a hundred years, so I paid homage to the tradition by creating my Bobbing Apple Punch, with miniature apples bobbing in bubbly spicy apple cider. If you are lucky enough to find spiced whole crabapples, use those real apples in place of the apple-shaped ice cubes!

**apple silicone mold suitable for ice cubes**
**2 750 ml bottles sparkling apple cider**
**4 quarts unfiltered fresh-pressed apple cider**
**spices to taste, pumpkin pie mix, etc**

Add red food coloring to a 1/2 cup of unfiltered apple cider with 1/2 cup water, then freeze in the apple silicone mold. Freezing all juice will never harden into an apple ice cube, and if you don't add coloring, the ice apples blend into the punch color. Unmold the ice apples, store in a plastic bag in the freezer, then use the mold to make ice apples until you have enough for your punch bowl or cauldron. Your ice apples will stay fine in the freezer for several weeks so make these well in advance.

Just before serving, pour unfiltered fresh-pressed apple cider and spices into a punch bowl or cauldron and stir so the spices are combined. Add the sparkling apple cider last to preserve the bubbles. Drop in some ice apples so as your party guests scoop their punch they see miniature bobbing apples!

I love thinking up new fun food of my own, but I also have fabulous friends who enjoy expressing their creativity. Since my parties have become so large it is difficult to prepare enough party food on my own, so I now have the Creepy Cuisine Contest each year. We have the benefit of potluck quantities of food, and my guests have a chance at the prestige of winning a prize for their creative efforts. Here are some of my favorite Creepy Cuisine Contest Champions. Thanks to everyone who granted permission to include their recipes!

# MANDARIN JACK O'LANTERNS

by Teje Vejrup

Most fruits and veggies can't be prepared until the day of the party, but you can make these adorable little Mandarin Jack O'Lanterns early! My friend Teje in Norway made these in 2013, so I mailed her a long-distance Creepy Cuisine trophy and was inspired to make some myself! I drew a slightly different face on 74 mandarins using a fine-tip black permanent marker, completely safe since it doesn't pass through the orange rind. I displayed them in see-through bowls like this wire one so everyone could see as many of the faces as possible. You could use full size oranges, but the mandarin oranges look more pumpkin shaped, some even still have stubby stems, they are much easier to peel, and they are a better size for finger food. These Mandarin Jack O'Lanterns last several weeks in the fridge, and since you just draw faces on the rinds with a black marker, these can be done plenty ahead of time…and an extra bonus is that they are a healthy treat!

# DEVILED EYES

by Dave & Wendy Taubler

I love deviled eggs, and there are many ways to make them spooky. Dave & Wendy dyed the yolks and hand-painted veins on the whites with olive garnish to make these bloody Deviled Eyes. Wendy says the basic recipe is just as tasty without the bloodshot effect for other events, and is easily doubled for a larger crowd.

6 hard-boiled eggs (separated into whites and yolks)
1/3 cup creme fraiche
1/4 crumbled, cooked bacon (optional)
1 teaspoon sriracha or other spicy asian chili sauce
1 tablespoon chopped cilantro
1/2 teaspoon spicy mustard
1/4 lime zest
1 teaspoon lime juice
salt to taste
red food coloring (to your color preference)
sliced black olives

Hardboil the eggs, slice lengthwise, and put all the yolks into a mixing bowl. Mash all ingredients except olives together with the cooked yolks and add food coloring until the yolks are the desired color. Spoon yolk mixture back into egg whites. Top each half with a sliced olive as the pupil. Dip a toothpick into the red food coloring and lightly draw "bloodshot" veins across the whites. Arrange on a tray and serve to horrified guests.

**TRICKS & TIPS**
See the Extras section for Creepy Cuisine Chef Cards to print for your own contest!

# MONSTER TOES

by Tracey Newport-Sholly

Tracey was inspired by an online recipe for mini pigs-in-blankets to make these Monster Toes. The olive toenails are the perfect touch with the green dough toes!

**biscuit dough (purchased or your favorite homemade dough)**
**green food coloring**
**melted butter**
**mini smoked sausages or cocktail franks**
**whole black olives, pitted**
**toothpicks**
**honey mustard or ketchup (optional)**

If you make your own biscuit dough, add 5 drops of green food coloring to your batter before you knead it into a light green dough. If you buy ready-made dough, tint the melted butter with green food coloring and brush the dough toes before baking.

Roll out your dough. Spread mustard or ketchup on the dough or you can reserve as dipping sauces. Cut dough into pieces large enough to cover one sausage, likely four per biscuit if using ready-made dough. Wrap the sausage in the dough, seal shut and place seam side down on a baking sheet. Cut a black olive in half. Push one half into the dough on the edge of the sausage. Use a toothpick to hold it in place as the toenail. Bake at 350 degrees for twenty minutes until they are golden green and ready for gnawing.

# FROSTED BAT WINGS AKA DEMENTED OWLS CHOCOLATE BACON

by Ruth Winter

Ruth won the prize for "Most Daring Culinary Risk" with her chocolate-covered bacon. The Frosted Bat Wings were white chocolate for the frosted effect, but normal chocolate works too. Not everyone enjoys salty meat with their chocolate, but I think this recipe is mighty tasty!

**Sliced raw bacon**
**White chocolate candy melts or milk chocolate**
**Decorating sugar flakes (optional)**

Fry up some bacon nice & crispy. Cool it for about 15 minutes and pat off excess grease. Cut the cooked bacon into 1-inch bits. Melt the chocolate per the package instructions, microwave is easiest not to burn. Dip the cooled bits of bacon into the chocolate to cover them. Put the chocolate covered bits of bacon on wax paper. Sprinkle some sugar flakes for sparkle, then put them into the fridge to completely cool and harden the chocolate. Serve to anyone brave enough to try!

**TRICKS & TIPS**
Milk chocolate and dark chocolate work just as well with bacon!

# SKONES WITH BLOOD RASPBERRY JAM

by Tracia Barbieri

Tracia found an oven-safe silicone skull pan on sale, so she cleverly thought of baking skull-shaped Skones! If you have your own favorite scone or biscuit recipe, it should work as long the dough is soft enough to take the shape of the pan while baking. Raspberry jam is a tasty way to add some bloody gore factor to an upper-crust British favorite.

**2 cups all-purpose flour**
**1/3 cup sugar**
**1 tsp baking powder**
**1/4 tsp baking soda**
**1/2 tsp salt**
**8 Tbsp (1/2 cup) unsalted butter, frozen**
**1/2 cup sour cream or plain yogurt (can be fat-free)**
**1 large egg**
**oven-safe skull pan – silicone is easiest to remove the Skones after baking**

Preheat oven to 400 degrees F. Mix dry ingredients in a medium bowl. Using the large holes on a box grater, grate butter into flour mixture. Use fingers to work butter into mixture until resembles coarse meal. Whisk sour cream and egg together in separate bowl until smooth, then add to flour mixture, stirring with fork until large dough clumps form. Use your hands to press the dough against the bowl into a ball. It may be sticky but the dough will eventually come together.

Spray the skull pan with non-stick cooking spray, even if using a silicone pan. Press dough into pan well so the dough will capture all the mold detail. Leave room for the dough to rise about a third higher. Bake until golden, about 15 minutes depending on the size of each mold. After baking, let cool in pans until shape is fully set, then unmold the Skones. Serve warm or at room temperature, over a bloodbath of raspberry jam.

# DECAPITARE PUMPKINUS EXPERIMENTI EXHIBITS A-J

by Lyle Seplowitz

Lyle was "experimenting" with miniature pumpkins, hence his name for this Creepy Cuisine Contest Winner. All the "decapitated" faces he drew had different personalities, and the yogurt parfait inside was absolutely delicious!

**2 cups plain non-fat (or low-fat) Greek yogurt**
**2 tbsp or 1 oz pureed pumpkin (canned or fresh)**
**4 tbsp or 2 oz 100% pomegranate juice**
**1/4 tsp pumpkin pie spice**
**small bowls, or hollowed out miniature pumpkins**

Hollow out miniature pumpkins out to use as bowls and draw faces on them in advance. Pour all the ingredients into a blender and mix until thoroughly combined. Taste for sweetness. Add agave nectar or honey if needed. Do not add more juice as this will make your yogurt too runny. Spoon the yogurt mixture into each pumpkin bowl. Top with either pumpkin seed granola or sliced fruit. Or both!

### TRICKS & TIPS
Experiment further by adding pumpkin seed granola, sliced fruit, or other ideas of your own!

# THE LAST TEMPTATION

by Lyle Seplowitz

*Lyle & Galt have brought many clever Creepy Cuisine entries over the years, and two have made it into my favorites! For The Last Temptation you can use your own favorite decadent bite-sized dessert recipe, but these clever descriptions made the presentation unique!*

The Last Temptation a la mode
Remove candy corn for The Original Sin
Abstinence is for priests
Abstemiousness gets you nothing
Eat one - don't be a FUSSBUDGET
PIETY is for PRIGS

**10 oz bittersweet chocolate, finely chopped
1 cup whipping cream
1 1/2 Tbsp Grand Marnier or other orange liqueur
1/4 cup orange marmalade
1/4 cup unsweetened cocoa powder (not Dutch-processed)
64 candy corns (about 3 oz)**

Line an 8x8-inch baking pan with a 12x17-inch sheet of foil or waxed paper. In a large heatproof bowl set over a saucepan of hot water, use a heatproof spatula or wooden spoon to stir together chocolate, cream, liqueur and marmalade until chocolate is melted. Scrape chocolate mixture into prepared pan, smoothing top. Chill until firm, at least 2 1/2 hours or up to 1 week covered with plastic wrap.

Put cocoa powder in a shallow bowl. Lift solid chocolate mixture from pan using edges of lining foil or paper. With a long sharp knife, cut chocolate mixture into 64 squares, each about ¾-inch wide. Roll squares in cocoa powder to coat, and place one square in each paper cup. Gently press a candy corn into the top of each truffle. Store between sheets of waxed paper in an airtight container in the fridge for up to 2 weeks. Be clever writing your own sinful descriptions to provide The Last Temptation to your guests!

# GLOWING & GLARING JACK O'LANTERN CHEESE BALL

by Glen Simon

Before he was named Ghoulish Glen, he arrived one year with his family's traditional delicious cheese spread formed into the cutest Glaring Jack O'Lantern Cheese Ball, so I dared him to make it glow next time. He succeeded and won the next year's Creepy Cuisine Contest hands down! Use the same basic cheese mixture for either the simpler and cute glaring one, or the impressively glowing face.

**16 oz (2 bricks) cream cheese**
**8 oz spreadable cheddar cheese (Kaukauna or similar)**
**2-3 oz crumbled blue cheese**
**1-2 tsp worcestershire sauce (to taste)**
**1 tbsp onion flakes**
**yellow & red food coloring**
**plastic wrap**
**small round bowl**
**pepper stem or broccoli stem**

Bring all the cheeses to room temperature. Use an electric mixer to combine all ingredients into a smooth pale orange mixture. Add a few drops of yellow & red food coloring and keep mixing until you have a nice pumpkin skin color. Choose your method to continue, either the simple solid pumpkin shape or the more advanced Glowing technique.

## GLARING JACK O'LANTERN CHEESE BALL

**Also need:**
**pretzel pieces or other edible items to create a face**

Spoon the cheese mixture into the center of a sheet of plastic wrap, pull the corners up and around to form a ball that can rest in the small round bowl. Twist all the extra plastic wrap together in a rope as tightly as possible, creating wrinkles for the grooved pumpkin skin texture. Once the rope is tight, let it twist into a knot, and press gently down into the top of the pumpkin, making the indentation for the stem. Chill at least 4-6 hours in the fridge for the cheese to set. Carefully remove the plastic wrap from the ball and set in place on the serving tray. The plastic wrap will stick a little to the cheese, making pock marks on the surface, but the grooves should stay intact. Use an offset spreader or butter knife to smooth the pocks on the surface but leave the grooves. Add either a pepper stem or a broccoli stem to be the pumpkin stem, and cut up a pretzel or using other edible items to create the adorable Glaring Jack O'Lantern Cheese Ball face.

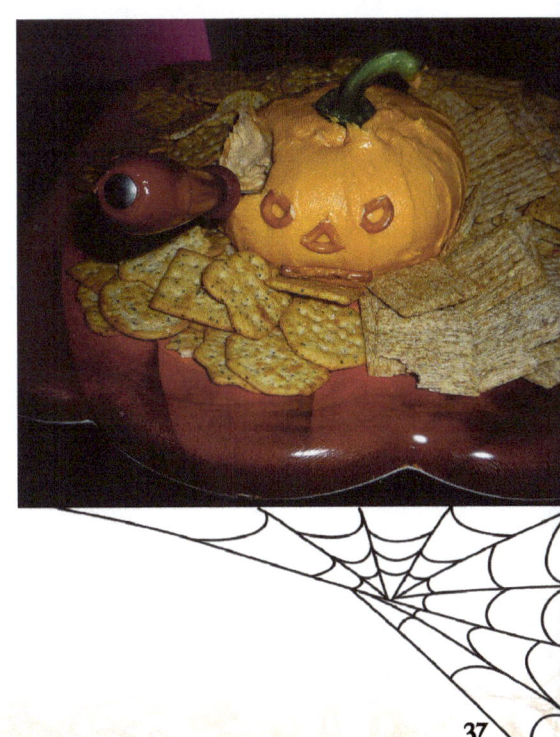

# GLOWING JACK O'LANTERN CHEESE BALL

**Also need:
round jar, juice glass or stemless wine glass
battery tealight
hard cheese in ½-inch thick slices (manchego, parmesan, etc)
strong skewer**

Select a small rounded jar, juice glass or stemless wine glass that can fit over the battery tealight and is large enough to hide inside your cheese ball. Cut the thick slices of hard cheese into the eyes & mouth shapes. Hold the jar from the inside while spreading the cheese around the back of the jar to the sides of the face area. Spread a thin layer of cheese mixture in the face area, press in the hard cheese eyes & mouth all the way to the jar surface, and spread enough mixture around to hold them in place. Keep spreading the cheese around the jar and between the facial features until you have a good thick layer around the jar in as round a shape as possible. You can use the plastic wrap technique from the previous Glaring version to create wrinkles, taking care not to disturb the facial features, or smooth the final surface and leave exposed to chill, which will result in a firmer surface but can dry out and crack if refrigerated too long. Even after covering the jar with a thick layer, you will have at least half of the cheese mixture left, so you can serve a pile of cheese on the same tray, or make smaller solid pumpkins using the Glaring technique.

After completely chilled at least 4-6 hours, hold the jar from the bottom opening again while using a strong skewer to pry out the cheese eyes & mouth without disturbing the cheese mixture around them. Smooth the facial openings, then set in place on the serving tray over the battery tealight. Remember to turn on the light first! Smooth the surface with an offset spreader or butter knife, then add either a pepper stem or a broccoli stem as the pumpkin stem, and appreciate the oohs and ahhs for the Glowing Jack O'Lantern Cheese Ball!

# Scary Savories

# SPICY BAT WINGS

This is another creative description of a familiar dish. Since I am not one for extremely spicy food, I used honey barbecue wings, but you can use spicy buffalo wings or your own spicy chicken wing recipe. Bats are a more obvious choice for Halloween, but these could be Gargoyle Wings or Raven Wings as well!

Bake purchased chicken wings according to the package instructions. Arrange and serve, making sure you have a sign to identify them as something spooky instead of just chicken!

# BATATO CHIPS

2 pounds purple potatoes, cut into 1/8-inch thick slices
3 tablespoons olive oil
coarse salt
(cayenne pepper to taste)
(ground pepper to taste)

Preheat oven to 400° F. Thinly slice purple potatoes on a mandolin slicer or cut carefully with a sharp knife. Use a metal cookie cutter to cut bat shapes out of the potato slices. A plastic cookie cutter will not be strong enough to cut through the raw potato. Lightly coat 2 rimmed baking sheets with cooking spray, set aside. Put potatoes, oil, 1 Tbsp salt (and cayenne if desired) in a large bowl, and season with pepper to taste. Toss to combine and completely coat the potatoes with oil. Place slices on prepared baking sheets at least 1/4-inch apart. Bake at 400° F for 7 minutes, then rotate the baking sheets and bake another 7 minutes. Chips should be crispy and curling slightly at the edges. Sprinkle with salt immediately while the chips are still on the baking sheets, then turn chips over onto parchment paper or paper towels to absorb excess oil. Use the leftover salt on the baking sheets to salt the other side of the chips, then let them cool and dry completely before serving.

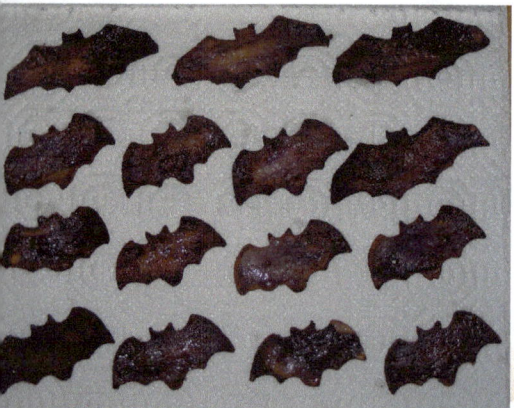

Look for purple potatoes at gourmet grocery stores or farmers markets. If you cannot find purple potatoes, you can use russet potatoes for albino bats or try soaking your potato slices in water tinted with food coloring of your choice, but your guests tongues will end up matching the food coloring. You can save your potato slice scraps and bake them with your chips, since they're tasty snacks as you're preparing for your party!

# SHAPELY SANDWICHES

sliced bread of your choice
sandwich filling of your choice
condiments of your choice
Halloween cookie cutters

Make your sandwiches however you'd like, but try to have ingredients that will stick together and not fall apart after the sandwiches have been cut. The metal cookie cutters work best, since not all the plastic ones are as tall to cut through all the bread and fillings.

I used turkey and cheddar cheese, ham and swiss cheese with just a little mayonnaise to moisten the bread, and herbed cheese spreads for my variety of sandwiches. I used a pumpkin cookie cutter for the ones shown.

# CREEPY CHEESE & CRACKERS

For 1999, I used a cookie stamp on melted American cheese while it was cooling in a flat cookie sheet. After it cooled thoroughly, I trimmed away the edges and had what you see at right. Since 2006 I usually have time to use my mini Halloween cookie cutters to cut the cheese shapes into white ghosts, orange pumpkins and white skulls.

# TRICKY CRAB TRIANGLES

one stick (1/2 cup) melted butter
one 6 1/2 oz can crab meat
1 small jar (approximately 5 oz) Kraft Old English cheese
1/2 cup mayonnaise
1/2 tsp. garlic salt
one package split English muffins

Combine first 5 ingredients, spread on muffins, put on cookie sheet and freeze. When frozen, cut each muffin into eight triangles. Put in plastic bag, return to freezer. When ready to use, put under broiler until bubbly. As you can see, these really aren't so tricky!

# FEROCIOUS FRUIT

I like to provide some healthy options in my Spooky Spreads of food, but how to give fruit and vegetables some spooky style? With menacing faces of course!

**Bosc pears**
**red apples**
**baby kiwi**
**your favorite fruits**

For carving faces, it is best to have contrasting skin compared to the inner fruit, like Bosc pears for their nice brown skin, or red apples. As long as you have one or two faces growling in the center, you can arrange the rest of your favorite fruit any way you like. If you are very lucky, you might find baby kiwi, since when cut in half across, they look like eyeballs! Remember that many fruits will turn brown when exposed to open air, so wait to carve until right before serving, or brush exposed areas with lemon juice to keep them from turning brown.

# VICIOUS VEGGIES

**red or orange peppers**
**jicama**
**celery**
**pearl onions**
**carrots**
**broccoli**
**your favorite vegetables**
**whole cloves**
**toothpicks**

Vegetables are a little more flexible than fruit since their cut surfaces last longer exposed to air, but they still won't last more than 24 hours without starting to change shape and wither. Jicamas are great because they have natural knobby faces you can enhance with your carving. Get inspired by the shapes you see, For instance, the curved corners of a red pepper can become devil horns. Cut pearl onions in half for googly eyes and poke a whole clove in the center for the pupil. Trim layers of white onions into teeth to add as a mouth. Break off toothpicks into smaller lengths to anchor pieces together. Celery tops can become beastly antlers, and spiky teeth are always scary!

# FRANKS-IN-STEINS

Sometimes a clever name creates a recipe you can't resist. These are basically pigs in blankets, a vintage classic appetizer, but by forming the dough differently and adding a pretzel handle, you have little Franks-In-Steins, perfect for your Halloween party!

If you can't find these mini franks, you can cut hot dogs into halves or thirds. I used homemade beer batter biscuit dough to go with the "stein" concept, but you could use canned biscuit dough as a shortcut. This biscuit recipe uses shortening & no dairy, but check your "franks" if your guests have dietary restrictions.

**mini sausages or cocktail "franks"**
**small hard pretzels**
**biscuit dough of your choice**

### BEER BISCUIT DOUGH

Yields 18 "steins" for mini franks

2 cups all-purpose flour
3 teaspoons baking powder
1 teaspoon salt
1/4 cup shortening
3/4 cup beer

Mix the flour, baking powder and salt together first in a food processor, then cut in 1/4 cup cold shortening. You can whisk the dry ingredients together then cut in the shortening by hand the old-fashioned way if you don't have a food processor. Once the dough is a cornmeal consistency, stir in the beer and knead lightly until the dough is no longer sticky.

Portion the dough into small balls and cover them to chill so they do not dry out. Dry off the mini franks with paper towels so the dough will not slide off. Prepare a silicone mat or greased baking sheet. Break the small pretzels apart so the two top loops can each be a handle. Quickly form a small ball of dough into a tall cup shape around the mini frank, flaring out the dough at the bottom. Stand the frank-filled dough stein on a greased or lined cookie sheet so it keeps a flat dough base at the bottom of the cup. Push a small hard pretzel into the seam side as the stein handle, squeezing the dough edges to seal around the pretzel so the dough does not pop open during baking. Repeat until all your Franks are in Steins.

Bake them at 450 F (230 C) until the biscuits are golden brown, usually less time than the original 10 minutes in the full-size biscuit recipe. Keep checking them along the way, since some of your steins might slouch during baking. If you prefer more color on the outside, you can use an egg wash or milk wash for more browning. Serve your Franks-In-Steins standing on a tray with some mustard for dipping and be ready for your guests to cheer Prost!

### TRICKS & TIPS

You can form all your biscuit steins around the mini sausages months ahead, freeze them baked, then reheat them the day of the party. These taste great warm or room temperature, but they might get scarfed before they cool down!

# VIOLENT VERTEBRAE

I was lucky enough to inherit the spine used in my great-grandparents' chiropractic practice, which is a fantastic prop for this recipe! As long as you arrange the rollups in the classic spinal curvature shape with the cheese discs between, you still have a lovely display of Violent Vertebrae!

**lavash bread or flour tortillas**
**your favorite cream cheese spread, like artichoke & spinach, etc**
**Colby cheese slices**
**round cutter same diameter as rollups**
**leaf lettuce (optional garnish)**

Spread a thin layer of the cream cheese mixture onto lavash bread or a flour tortilla. Lavash bread is rectangular so there is less wasted after cutting into slices. Roll carefully so the cheese isn't squeezed out but tightly enough that the cheese glues the bread into a roll. Find a round cutter that is the same diameter as your finished roll. Roll foil tightly around and chill until set enough to slice. You can quick-chill in the freezer, but frozen solid is too hard to slice. Repeat for additional rolls, since more is better as these are scarfed quickly during the party.

While the rolls are chilling, use the round cutter to cut discs from the Colby cheese. If you can't find Colby cheese or would like to use something different, find a cheese with enough color to show up against the white rollups. Save the cheese discs in plastic bags in the fridge so they do not dry out.

After the rolls are chilled enough, slice into large spine-sized rolls at least as long as they are wide. Arrange on the serving tray in a curve with a cheese disc between each roll as the spinal discs between the vertebrae. A large silver oval serving tray lined with leaf lettuce is the perfect amount of elegance for contrast when serving a spine. Voila, Violent Verterbrae!

# Dastardly Desserts

# SNEAKY SLICES WITH GOLDEN GOO

sliced apples
purchased caramel dipping sauce
(not ice cream topping)

A spin on a traditional Halloween treat of caramel apples without all the mess! Cut the apples into slices if not already. Pre-sliced apples can be purchased now in snack-size bags, which are not only a time-saver, but they have been treated with citric acid so will not turn brown.

# MAGICAL MANDRAKES

Real mandrake roots look suspiciously like deformed babies, and have been used throughout the centuries in magical or herbal preparations. These mandrake seedlings are completely safe to eat, no ear protection required!

1 lb jar (2 cups) all natural "old-fashioned" peanut butter
1 cup powdered sugar
1 cup graham cracker crumbs
fresh celery stalk tops with leaves intact, soaked in cold water for a few hours
chocolate candy rocks (optional)
chocolate cookie crumbs for "dirt"
drinking straws cut in half
small shot glasses or large glass container for serving

Drain the oil from the top of the jar of peanut butter. Mix drained peanut butter with powdered sugar and graham cracker crumbs with a spoon well to form peanut butter clay. Mixture will be crumbly until you knead it with your hands. Refrigerate until ready to shape. Bring to room temperature and knead again. Once smooth in texture, mold into desired shape of a crying baby. Insert a drinking straw carefully into the top of the head down into the body, and leave the straw in place while the clay is chilling so the stem hole doesn't collapse. Repeat until all mandrakes are prepared. Can store chilled for several days before serving.

When ready to serve, remove the straw, pat dry a celery leaf stalk, then insert the celery into the hole using fresh peanut butter as glue, with the leaves coming out the top. Put small candy rocks in the bottom of a small clear plastic glass, add chocolate cookie crumb "dirt" halfway, tilting the glass so the dirt is along the side, insert the baby mandrake, then fill with more dirt crumbs.

# TOOTH DECAY FODDER

This is my attempt to make even one of the best parts of Halloween scary by naming it with the possible consequences of overindulgence.

Arrange your favorite Halloween candy in a bowl or coffin. I prefer classic candy corn in a large skull bowl.

# PUMPKIN PASTIES

Inspired by a popular children's book series and now one of the most popular items on my Halloween menu, these tasty treats put traditional pumpkin pie into bite-sized packages as perfect appetizers.

**Yields about 3 dozen miniature pasties**

2 eggs, slightly beaten
3/4 cup sugar
1 lb can pumpkin
(or 2 cups fresh, roasted in the oven then strained)
1/2 tsp salt
1 tsp cinnamon
1/2 tsp ginger
1/4 tsp cloves
1 2/3 cups evaporated milk (1 can)
1/2 tsp allspice
9 oz pie crust pastry (enough for two single standard pie crusts)

Bake the pie filling only (no crust) in a large greased casserole dish in hot oven (425° F) for 15 minutes. Keep oven door closed and reduce temp to moderate (350° F) and continue baking for 45 minutes or until table knife inserted in center of dish comes out clean. Cool on wire rack.

Make or purchase pie crust pastry. Roll thin and cut into circles approximately 4" in diameter. Put a spoonful of the cooled pumpkin mixture towards one side of the center of the circle. Fold over the crust into a half-circle and firmly crimp the edges closed. Place on a greased cookie sheet, slice three small slits in the top for venting, and bake only until crust is a light golden-brown. The pumpkin filling will begin to make the crust soggy when stored over time, so these are best baked the day of serving. These can be made ahead by freezing the assembled pasties unbaked on cookie sheets, then thawed and baked the day of serving. Great served at room-temperature, then you don't have to worry about your guests possibly burning their mouths from the steaming hot pumpkin inside!

### TRICKS & TIPS
You can save some time by purchasing pie crust pastry dough, but check the ingredients against any special dietary needs, since often they use lard or butter.

# DONUT BE SCARED PEEKABOO PUMPKINS

I have been working on recipes for see-through jack o'lantern shapes with pumpkin flavors for several years now. I recently acquired the family deep fryer, so I was finally successful with this recipe for 3 dozen mini donuts. I used a flying bat cutter upside-down as a spiky grin. I made this recipe vegan by using some simple substitutions that I have included, and they are just as delicious as the original recipe. I prefer them with a brighter orange icing or a little sparkle, but they can be served plain as well. These pumpkin donuts are easy, adorable and tasty, so Donut Be Scared!

3 1/2 cups all-purpose flour
4 tsp baking powder
1 tsp salt
2 tsp ground cinnamon
1 tsp ground ginger
1/2 tsp baking soda
1/2 tsp ground nutmeg
1/4 tsp ground cloves
1 cup sugar
3 Tbsp unsalted butter, room temperature
    (or non-dairy baking margarine)
1 large egg plus 2 egg yolks (or 2 "eggs" of vegan egg replacer)
1 tsp vanilla extract
1/2 cup + 1 Tbsp buttermilk (or water)
1 cup canned pure pumpkin (or 1.5 cups fresh pumpkin puree)
canola oil (for deep-frying)

Whisk first 8 dry ingredients in medium bowl to blend. Using electric mixer, beat sugar and room-temperature butter in large bowl until blended (mixture will be grainy). Beat in egg, then extra yolks and vanilla. If using fresh pumpkin puree that has more moisture than canned pumpkin, do not add buttermilk or water. Gradually beat in buttermilk if needed. Beat in one fourth of pumpkin at a time. Using rubber spatula, fold in dry ingredients in 4 additions, blending gently after each addition. Cover with plastic; chill at least 3 hours.

Sprinkle 2 rimmed baking sheets lightly with flour, even if you are using a silicone mat. Press out 1/3 of dough on floured surface to 1/2- to 2/3-inch thickness. Cut donut shapes either using 2 1/2-inch-diameter round cutter or pumpkin cutters and arrange on flour-dusted sheets. For jack o'lanterns, cut the outer pumpkin shape, arrange on sheets, then cut out the eyes & mouth after on the sheet. Drinking straws or mini triangle cutters work well for eyes, and an upside-down flying bat works well for a mouth. Repeat with remaining dough in

2 more batches. Chill dough scraps with remaining dough before rolling again. Prep one dozen from 1/3 of dough, put scraps in to chill while frying this dozen, then roll the next dozen.

Line 2 baking sheets with several layers of paper towels. Fill and heat deep fryer, or pour oil into large deep skillet to depth of 1 1/2 inches. Attach deep-fry thermometer and heat oil to 365°F to 370°F. Gently lower the jack o'lantern shape into the oil so the face does not distort. As soon as shape is set, flip over or one side will crack while frying. Fry donuts, 3 or 4 at a time, until golden brown, adjusting heat to maintain temperature, about 1 minute per side. Using slotted spoon or tongs, transfer to paper towels to drain. Cool completely before decorating. Can be frozen undecorated for 1-2 weeks and reheated in a low-temperature oven the morning of the party. See, I told you, Donut Be Scared!

# ORANGE PUMPKIN ICING

1 1/2 cups powdered sugar
2 Tbsp pumpkin juice (or water)
yellow & red food coloring
orange sugar (optional)

When I roast my fresh pumpkin and strain it into puree, I save the pumpkin juice leftover from straining. You can use that for this icing for an extra boost of pumpkin goodness or use plain water. Mix the liquid and powdered sugar until smooth. Add yellow and red food coloring until you have a nice bright pumpkin orange color. Icing should be thin enough to find its own level when spreading onto donuts but not drip into the holes or off the sides. Add orange sugar while icing is still wet for extra sparkle.

**TRICKS & TIPS**
Some simple vegan substitutions are just as delicious as the original. Donut Be Scared to experiment!

# FOOLPROOF SUGAR COOKIES

Rolled cookies with cookie cutters are a staple for all holidays, and can become ghosts, pumpkins, black cats, gargoyles, skulls, or gravestones just by finding the right cutter shape. This sugar cookie recipe from my aunt has proven itself over the years as foolproof, as well as being only sweet enough so that their flavor supports sweet icing nicely. These are easily made non-dairy by using non-dairy margarine and water instead of butter and milk, and even vegan by using egg-replacer powder.

**Yields 5 or 6 dozen standard cookie cutter shapes**

2 cups margarine or butter
2 1/4 cups sugar
3 eggs
1 1/2 teaspoon vanilla
6 cups flour
3/4 teaspoon salt
4 tablespoons milk (can use water)

Cream sugar into softened butter, then mix in eggs, salt and vanilla, adding flour last. Only add milk or water if the dough is too dry. These are easily made vegan using vegan margarine and egg-replacer powder. Chill 1 hour. Unbaked mixed dough can be refrigerated for at least one week before baking. Roll out one-sixth of dough 1/8 to 1/4 inch thick and cut with cookie cutter of your choice. Place on a greased cookie sheet and bake at 375º F (190º C) for 12 minutes. If making different shapes, group similar size shapes on the same sheets for even baking. These can be frosted. After icing is completely dry, these can be stored in an airtight container for at least two weeks or longer.

### TRICKS & TIPS
The Foolproof Sugar Cookies are perfect for making Edible Medals & Tasty Tombstones!

# BUTTERCREAM FROSTING

Thanks to Kathy Henricks for her tried & true frosting recipe! This frosting is perfect for icing cakes and hand-spreading onto cookies since it stays soft.

1 1/4 cup Crisco shortening (only use Crisco)
2 lbs powdered sugar
1 teaspoon salt
1/2 cup water
2 tablespoons light corn syrup
1 teaspoon butter flavoring
1 teaspoon vanilla

Beat 5 to 10 minutes with a power mixer until very smooth. Water down a small amount for a crumb coat if frosting a cake. After 20 minutes (when set), frost with remainder of frosting. When set, use paper towel or typing paper to set desired surface texture. This is fluffy enough to spread easily with a knife onto cakes or cookies, yet stiff enough for keeping its shape for piping and decorating.

# ROYAL ICING

This is the traditional recipe that glues gingerbread houses together or makes a hard candy-like surface on cookies or cakes. Use this recipe for the Startling Spiders and the Ghoulish Gravestones. If you are making spiders and icing cookies with Royal Icing, make one large batch, tint gray, reserve about 1 cup in another bowl for your spiders and tightly cover. Thin the rest of the icing with corn syrup for smoothly-iced cookies, then you still have your stiff Royal Icing ready to be tinted black for spiders!

**Makes enough to ice 5-6 dozen sugar cookies**

16 oz powdered sugar
3 egg whites
1/2 tsp cream of tartar

Beat until peaks firmly hold their shape, the more you beat it, the firmer the frosting. This hardens when exposed to air, but dissolves in water, so keep a moist towel over the bowl while working with it. Use a tight-fitting plastic container to store in the refrigerator for a couple weeks, but the egg whites begin to separate from the sugar any longer than that. Hard royal icing decorations like spiders can last indefinitely if kept away from moisture. If you are concerned about using raw egg whites, you can purchase pasteurized eggs, or you can use meringue powder found at specialty baking stores.

## TRICKS & TIPS
Use Royal Icing for a hard candy-like surface for painting, but Buttercream Frosting for a soft sweet spreadable that can still stack for storage.

# EDIBLE MEDALS

Over the many years of my party hosting career, I realized that many winners of my party contests didn't want the prizes or trophies, so I thought to make Edible Medals instead. That way the winner still has the public recognition at the party and a photo to remember the moment, but they can also enjoy chomping the cookie!

I like the classic simplicity of the circle medal, but you can cut any shape you like. Roll your dough no thinner than 1/4 inch, and don't forget to cut a hole in each cookie before baking for threading the ribbon. I use my Foolproof Sugar Cookie recipe for my Edible Medal dough since it holds its shape, doesn't spread, and is easily made vegan for more guests to enjoy. You can try using rice flour for a gluten-free version, but it will be more fragile so might break off the ribbon.

Being able to print with food coloring on edible sheets has inspired me for many new creations, including so many different realistic embossed designs for my Edible Medals, but you do not need an edible printer to make them! You can bake the cookies, frost them with a flat floodcoat of Royal Icing, making sure you don't clog the hole with icing, then after the royal icing is solid, use piping tips with contrasting icing or food coloring pens to write your awards, like 1st, 2nd, 3rd, Best Costume, etc. You could even pipe or write directly on the baked cookie if you like the raw rustic look or add food coloring to the dough.

I have not yet figured out how to make the ribbon edible without sticking to hair, skin or clothing, or breaking under the weight of the cookie, so I use normal ribbon to hang the medal ceremoniously around the winner's neck. Thinner ribbon is easier to work with, and now there are many festive styles for every possible holiday, but 1-inch ribbon looks more like a medal, and you can roll the 1-inch ribbon end to fit through the cookie hole. You must be gentle and slow threading the ribbon through the hole or you could crack your cookie, so I always make a few spares just in case. I pull only enough ribbon through the hole to tie the knot behind the medal so the knot is hidden and there is less stress on the cookie. Making the cookie thicker with the hole not too close to the edge helps prevent breakage. You may store your Edible Medals in airtight tins for at least two weeks so you can make them well in advance for your party. Now you too can make your own Edible Medals for any contest you can imagine!

# GHOULISH GRAVESTONES

For the Ghoulish Gravestone cookies, use the Foolproof Sugar Cookies recipe with a gravestone cookie cutter, bake and cool completely, then cover with Royal Icing. The buttercream frosting is too soft for these cookies since you cannot write on the surface of the frosting. Tint the icing gray using a small amount of black food coloring, then add just enough light corn syrup for the icing to level itself when spread, but so it still hardens enough to use food coloring pens for the lettering. Be sure to wait a full day or at least overnight for the royal icing to harden completely before using the food coloring pens. Food coloring pen sets have become available in most large grocery stores with the cake decorating supplies, plus specialty cake decorating stores or online. If you cannot find any, use a fine, soft watercolor brush and normal black food coloring.

You can use any lettering style you like for your gravestone epitaphs, and you can vary your font styles as you wish. If you are overwhelmed by the concept of free-hand lettering, print out your epitaphs from your computer in fonts you like and the layout centered to your preference, then use those as models to draw on the cookies. I say "draw" because elaborate lettering by hand is much more like drawing than writing, since you are placing each line for the end result image, not just writing quickly to get words down.

I hadn't made gravestone cookies in the past since the only cookie cutters I found were the simple upside-down U shape, which I thought too boring, but I found a more elaborate cutter the same year I made my first outside gravestone decorations, so I thought the theme very appropriate! My first year I wanted to be sure the epitaphs were legible so everyone would get the jokes, which they did, and I was going for a simple carved style. The next year I kicked myself because I've been good at free-hand calligraphy since I was 9 years old, so why not go all out with the lettering? I chose a consistent Old English blackletter font style since I liked the look and can do it in my sleep since I've done it free-hand so many years now. Since I hadn't used the "punny" epitaphs for my yard gravestones, I used them on my cookies, using the same 13 epitaphs that made me laugh the most for the entire batch of cookies. The only drawback to making these cookies every year is that in only 4 years my black food coloring pen ran out of ink!

# TASTY TOMBSTONES

In 2011 I finally invested in an edible printer, and the first design I printed were Tasty Tombstones, using photos of my handcarved and painted foam gravestones but digitally replacing the carved epitaphs with my favorite punny names. When I saw how they came out, I clapped my hands & squealed in delight! You can purchase these printed frosting sheets in sets of 13 cookies from my BrittaBlvd Etsy shop as the punny epitaphs, blank epitaphs, or custom epitaphs of your choice.

Frosting sheets can be used to decorate cakes, cupcakes, frosting and fondant, or even baked directly on the cookie surface if you use shortbread or any cookie recipe that does not spread or rise during baking. Otherwise use corn syrup to glue the frosting sheet to the plain baked cookie, or place the frosting sheet on a layer of frosting. Store your frosting sheets in the zip bag provided out of direct light to prevent fading. Best used within one year. The sheet lasts better intact for storage, so do not cut out the shapes until just before using on your baked goods. Cut frosting sheet shapes and store in plastic zip bags no earlier than a few days before baking. The recipes included in your order, including my Foolproof Sugar Cookies, have been tested with many batches of frosting sheets and all work well for minimal spread or cracking.

To bake frosting sheet shapes directly on cookies, roll or pat dough to 1/8th inch thick directly onto parchment paper or use a silicone baking mat. Unpeel the cut frosting sheet shape from the backing and place onto the rolled dough. If the sheets begin to rip, chill in the fridge for a couple minutes before unpeeling. Leave about 1 inch baking space between cookies when placing the frosting sheet shapes. Since these stones are all different shapes, use the frosting sheet edge as a guide to cut around the shape with a dull knife so not to cut the surface below the cookies. Remove excess dough leaving the cookies in place, and repeat until the tray is filled. Pat gently to ensure the frosting sheet has good contact around the edges and entire surface of the cookie, then bake per the recipe instructions. Remove from oven and immediately tap down any bubbles with an oven mitt while the cookies are still hot. Allow cookies to cool completely on the sheet before transferring to a cooling rack.

I like to tint my cookie dough gray to match the printed frosting sheet, especially when displaying thicker Tasty Tombstones standing up in cookie crumb dirt like a graveyard, but you can also easily arrange thinner cookies flat on trays, especially if they are clues for one of your party mysteries!

# Spooky Spiders & Skeletons

# STARTLING SPIDERS

These edible spiders are made from Royal Icing in the previous chapter, which needs to be used right away since it hardens to a rocklike texture very quickly! Mix up the Royal Icing per the recipe, and add black gel food coloring to get the mixture as dark as you can. It will dry a darker color than your wet icing looks. I only made a third of the Royal Icing recipe and I still had a lot of icing leftover after making two dozen spiders.

These are very fragile, especially when peeling them off the waxed paper, since the legs tend to break off. Place gently around your party table for a spooky look, but if you place near moisture, you might have a black food coloring mess that will be difficult to clean! I used a decorating cone with plain round writing tip to pipe the icing into spider shapes on waxed paper.

At the left and right are finished spiders, then left to right shows what I pipe on a sheet of waxed paper. I pipe the legs first, then plop on a small round blob for the head, then I make sure the outside edge of the body touches all the legs, then fill it in with a bigger blob for the body to stand up higher than the head or legs.

If your hand gets sore from piping spiders like mine does, put a toothpick in the piping tube nozzle so the icing doesn't dry and plug the nozzle. Taking breaks is good since the warmer the icing gets, the bigger and sloppier your lines become, so let the icing bag rest back to room temperature, then keep piping away until you get sick of spiders! For me that's usually about 3 dozen, or one cookie sheet full, and usually happens over the course of several days while watching TV and waiting for other Halloween recipes to set or bake. Once the spiders are dry, as long as they stay away from moisture, they will keep indefinitely.

### TRICKS & TIPS
If your hand gets sore from piping spiders like mine does, put a toothpick in the piping tube nozzle and take a break!

# "SPIDERS OF THE SEA" BLACK RICE CRAB CAKES

These tasty crab cakes use black rice and orange cheddar cheese for an elegant Halloween treat! Serve in mini spiderweb design cupcake papers for some extra spooky style at your party buffet, or serve full size for a dastardly delicious dinner.

**to cook rice:**
1 cup water or chicken broth
1 cup rice, uncooked

2 cups cooked black rice
2 eggs
12 oz crabmeat, drained & flaked
1/4 cup grated parmesan cheese
1/4 grated cheddar & jack cheese mix
1 teaspoon garlic salt
(1/4 cup butter or margarine for sautéing only)

Prepare black rice per the package instructions, using 1 cup of chicken broth instead of water if desired. 1 cup uncooked rice should yield 2 cups cooked. Let the rice cool then fluff with a fork. Rice can be made in advance and refrigerated up to a week.

Beat 2 eggs in a large bowl. Add 2 cups cooked and cooled black rice, 12 oz crabmeat and grated cheeses, then mix lightly to combine. Chill for ingredients to set firmly for portioning.

For party size mini crab cakes, use a small disher scoop to portion the chilled mixture onto a silicone baking mat or parchment paper baking sheet, then shape each gently into a patty. Freeze uncooked until solid, then you can store in zip bags in the freezer before thawing and baking the day of your event. If baking right away, let stand 5 minutes for shape to set. Bake at 350F 5 minutes on each side, or until heated through and lightly browned on both sides. Makes 24 servings using a larger disher, can stretch to 48 servings approx 1.5" diameter using a smaller disher.

For dinner portions, shape full batch into 8 patties. Let stand 5 minutes for shape to set. Melt 1/4 cup butter in a large skillet on medium heat. Add patties; cook 5 minutes on each side, or until heated through and lightly browned on both sides.

# SLIMY SPIDERS

Cream cheese can be sculpted into almost anything and it goes well with crackers and many creative and colorful sauces. I'd been making my bloody red chili sauce Sinister Skulls for years, so for my big spider year, I decided to change up the colors and shapes by making Slimy Spiders!

**plastic wrap**
**1 medium spider cookie cutter (optional)**
**1 package cream cheese**
**1 jar green jalapeño jelly**
**crackers for spreading**

This is more edible art than a full recipe since the only ingredients are softened cream cheese and some sort of edible green slime! I had a medium size spider cookie cutter, but you can use a table knife to cut your spider shape free hand.

Line a sheet of foil with plastic wrap, enough of both to wrap entirely around your final cream cheese spider. Spoon about half a block of softened cream cheese into the spider cookie cutter, pressing firmly to force the cream cheese into all the legs. Gently remove the cookie cutter, pushing down on the feet in hopes the legs will not break. Make any leg repairs while forming them into a rounder shape. Add more cream cheese to build up the head and abdomen, then smooth everything with a table knife or offset spatula so it all holds together.

Fold the plastic wrap over the top so the cheese doesn't dry out, fold the foil over to protect the shape, especially the legs, then place in the fridge to chill to set firmly. They will stay a few weeks fine in the fridge, and you can freeze them for a few days, but freezing them too long causes the cheese to crumble after it thaws.

When ready to serve, place half a block of cream cheese in your serving dish first, then gently place the cream cheese spider on the block of cream cheese to keep the legs in place. This might be easier by holding the spider in your palm with the bottom facing out, then adding to the block of cream cheese before placing everything in the serving dish. Add bright green jalapeño jelly to the dish, carefully spooning the slime into all the crevices between the spider legs, covering all the base cream cheese. Serve with crackers and a spreader for everyone to enjoy your Slimy Spiders!

# SPIDERWEB BRIE EN CROUTE

Wrap a packaged puff pastry sheet around a small round of Brie cheese, sealing the raw edges together underneath. Use the leftover pastry scraps to add your own design to the top of the Brie, gluing on the pastry with water, milk or egg wash. Cookie cutters might give you inspiration, or roll your scraps into thin ropes and make a spiderweb design. Brush with milk or egg wash for nice browning. Place on greased foil on a cookie sheet and bake in the oven at 400º F for 15 minutes, or until crust is golden brown. Serve with a spreader and your preferred assortment of crackers.

You can leave your Brie en Croute plain which is still tasty, or you can add a layer between the pastry and the Brie if you like. My favorites are my homemade spiced loquat jam, or apricot preserves with dried cranberries. Any large chunks of fruit make the pastry surface lumpy, so that could mar your design if your work is intricate.

### TRICKS & TIPS
Any large chunks of fruit make the pastry surface lumpy, so that could mar your design if your work is intricate.

# FRIED SPIDERS

Inspired by the traditional Cambodian delicacy, in 2003 I tried making my own Fried Spiders out of pre-made ingredients. These are quite fragile but tasty!

**For each fried spider:**
1 frozen breaded cream-cheese-filled jalapeño popper
4 frozen ready-to-bake breaded onion rings
egg wash
wooden toothpicks soaked in water

Soak the wooden toothpicks for at least 30 minutes. Thaw the ready-to-bake jalapeño poppers and onion rings enough to be able to use toothpicks and knives on them. Cut the onion rings in half to make the curved legs. Attach the 8 legs to the jalapeño pepper body with egg wash and hold in place with the wet toothpicks. Bake in the oven according to the jalapeño popper package instructions, taking care not to burn the legs. Carefully arrange on a serving platter, since the legs might fall off, just like real fried spiders!

# FAL-AWFUL ARACHNIDS HOMEMADE FALAFEL

As Ghoulish Glen and I were brainstorming more spider-themed party food, he came up with "Fal-Awful Arachnids" as spider-shaped homemade falafel! Fair warning that these are a multi-day process that will take time and patience, but the result is a beautifully brown savory spider with a satisfying crunch around a creamy center, and even vegan and gluten-free!

**Yields 18 tarantula-size spiders**

2 cups dried chickpeas
1 Tbsp ground cumin
1 Tbsp ground coriander
3 cloves garlic, minced (or through a garlic press)
1 small yellow onion, chopped, or 1/4 cup dried minced onion
1 cup packed fresh cilantro leaves
1 cup packed fresh parsley leaves
zest of 1 lemon
1/4 tsp cayenne pepper
1 1/2 tsp salt, plus more in a shaker for liberal seasoning after frying
1/2 tsp black pepper
canola oil for frying

Place chickpeas in a large bowl and fill with water to cover them to a depth of 3 inches. Cover the bowl with plastic wrap and leave on counter for 24 hours. The chickpeas will triple in size and absorb quite a bit of the water so check a few times during soaking to see if you need to add more water. Once the beans have soaked for 24 hours, drain and rinse well.

Place the drained chickpeas, ground spices, garlic, onion, cilantro, and parsley into a food processor, then pulse carefully until everything has been ground. Do not overgrind into a paste.

Mix the lemon zest, cayenne, salt, and black pepper into the ground chickpeas then roll a small amount of the mixture into a walnut sized ball or a small patty with your hands. The mixture should hold together nicely and not fall apart.

Once your dough is complete, you are ready to form shapes. Place a spider cookie cutter on a parchment-lined baking sheet or silicone mat. Do not use wax paper since the falafel will stick when frozen. Firmly pat the falafel mixture into the cookie cutter, then carefully remove the cookie cutter, helping the legs stay on the sheet by gently poking them with a skewer. If any legs break, repair them with your fingers, tightly packing the dough together. Scrape any extra dough away from the edges, then roll two balls, one for the abdomen and

## TRICKS & TIPS

The best falafels start with dried chickpeas, not canned, so we bought one full bag online that made 3 and a half batches, yielding about 5 dozen tarantula-sized spiders, plenty for a party crowd!

the other for the head, pressing them into the spider shape with no seams. Repeat until your dough is gone, then place in the freezer for at least 2 hours until frozen solid. We did try using the cookie cutter on a flat sheet of falafel dough, but that was a much worse mess!

Check your frozen falafel spiders by carefully prying them off the non-stick surface in advance of frying, since you can repair breakage and refreeze. Once they are loose from the non-stick surface, they are much easier to manage to get into the fryer.

When you are ready to fry, pour oil in a Dutch oven, a large, high-sided skillet, or a deep fryer to a depth of 2-3 inches, enough to cover the falafel. Place a thermometer into the oil and heat over med-high heat until the temperature reaches 360° - 375° F.

While the oil is heating place a flattened paper grocery bag onto a baking sheet and cover with a few clean paper towels. Place a baking rack upside-down over the paper towels. This will help to collect the oil as it drains off of your falafel.

When the oil is up to temperature, fry a test falafel. The oil should bubble up and sizzle all around it. The falafel itself should stay together in one piece and not break apart at all. Since the dough is frozen solid to keep its shape, it should take about 4 minutes to fry to a beautiful golden brown, but your frying time will depend on the size spider you make. Our tarantula size took about 4 minutes to fry, flipping once to brown both sides since they tend to float. Keep the remaining falafel in the freezer until the fryer is ready for more. Remove the cooked falafel from the oil and drain on the prepared baking sheet. Sprinkle with coarse salt while the falafel is still hot. Fry the remaining falafel in batches, being careful to not overcrowd the oil which drops the temperature.

We didn't toast our spices, and dried minced onions worked fine, but do not skip the lemon zest since it really makes a difference in flavor. Our tiny deep fryer only had room to fry two spiders, and it was easiest to stagger the timing, so the first spider was set before the next spider entered the frying oil. Do keep them warm while serving to your guests. We heated an aluminum cauldron and dishtowel in the oven to keep our spiders warm, and they didn't get soggy, but the warmth only lasted an hour or two, not the entire party.

Serve your spiders immediately while still warm, or to make ahead, only flash-fry to set the shape, store in the freezer, then bake at 350F/160C to thaw completely and recrisp them just before serving. These taste best when warm, not room temperature, so use a heat lamp or a dry chafing dish to keep them warm during your party so your guests can fully appreciate your Fal-Awful Arachnids!

# TASTY TARANTULAS SPIDER ROSETTES

Longtime Eerie Elegance fans might remember that I've been trying to make savory Fried Spiders for years, with moderate success since they were very fragile and many fell apart on the display tray. You can find my original Fried Spiders on the previous page, and another savory version as Fal-Awful Arachnids. When I saw a spider rosette form for sale on Amazon, I absolutely had to try making some! See the Eerie Elegance Eats Extras section in the back of this book for the Amazon link, but buy it when you see it, since it often goes out of stock! You can often find other holiday rosette forms like pumpkins and cats, so you can adapt the colors and flavors in this recipe to the shapes you'd like to make.

I have enjoyed eating rosettes many Christmases in my life since they are a popular Scandinavian holiday treat, but I had never tried making them before. Luckily I have a friend Kathy who is the Rosette Queen, so I asked her advice and she graciously replied with her secrets. I used her tried and true recipe and tips, replacing the eggs and milk with vegan substitutes and added a couple drops of black gel food coloring while mixing in my blender that is older than I am. After frying them in the deep fryer also older than me, then sprinkling them with fine black sanding sugar instead of powdered sugar, we had adorable fuzzy, black, crispy, fried, Tasty Tarantulas!

Be prepared for several hours of work in one session, since you are frying each spider individually for 2-3 minutes, sprinkling sugar over the completed spider while reheating the metal form bare in the oil, then repeating, so it took about 5 hours for us to make almost 9 dozen Tasty Tarantulas from only two batches of batter. I was so glad that my friend Angie volunteered to help, since she had a nostalgic blast back to when she and her mom would make Christmas rosettes in North Dakota!

### TRICKS & TIPS
Use a container only slightly larger than your iron shape for less waste. Even though we had the perfect size flat-bottom dish, I still had a layer of batter that refused to stick to the iron when it got too low…and the hot iron cooked the spider in the dish!

# TASTY TARANTULAS SPIDER ROSETTES

**Yields about 4 to 5 dozen rosettes**

2 eggs, slightly beaten (or equivalent vegan egg replacer)
1 cup milk (or rice milk)
2 teaspoons granulated sugar
1 cup all-purpose flour
1/4 teaspoon salt
1 tablespoon vanilla extract (or almond or lemon)
couple drops black gel food coloring
canola oil or vegetable oil for frying

Add eggs (or egg replacer) first in blender and mix well. Add sugar and milk then mix again. Sift flour before measuring into blender, then add salt and mix again until batter is smooth and about the consistency of heavy cream. Add flavoring and food coloring. Let the batter rest for about 30 minutes in a flat-bottomed shallow container large enough to fit the rosette iron form, but only slightly larger than your iron form shape for less waste. While the mixture is resting, heat the frying oil to 375F, either in a heavy pan or deep fryer. Oil should be hot enough to brown a piece of bread while counting sixty.

Once the frying oil is up to temperature, dip the rosette iron into the hot oil to heat it for at least two minutes, then drain excess oil on paper towel. Dip heated iron in batter to not more than three-fourths its height. If only a thin layer of batter adheres to the iron, dip it again until a smooth layer forms. It will be partly cooked, from the heat of the iron. Plunge batter-coated iron quickly into the hot oil and cook from two to three minutes until active bubbling ceases. Remove from iron and drain on paper towels. If the spider does not release on its own, use a table knife to gently push it off the iron. Immediately put the iron back into the oil to reheat, then sprinkle the finished rosette with granulated sugar. If your rosettes are not crisp, then the batter is too thick, and should be diluted with milk.

As long as they are kept in a good airtight cookie tin with wax paper between layers, your Tasty Tarantulas last over two weeks still crispy and tasty...but fair warning that all the black food coloring will make your lips and tongue black!

# THE GARGANTULA CHEESE BALL

Ghoulish Glen first brought his family cheese ball recipe to my Halloween party with a cute little jack o'lantern face, then plussed it the following year by making it glow, winning a Creepy Cuisine award both years. For our spider menu, we thought we could make the cheese ball recipe into a giant spider using real crab legs, and Scary Jerry brilliantly thought of covering the cheese ball with black sesame seeds...voila the Gargantula!

16 ounces (2 bricks) cream cheese
8 ounces spreadable cheddar cheese (Kaukauna or similar)
2-3 ounces crumbled blue cheese
1-2 teaspoons worcestershire sauce (to taste)
1 tablespoon onion flakes
plastic wrap

black sesame seeds
black gel food coloring & food-safe brush
8 cooked crab legs still in shells, preferably from the same crab to be symmetrical
8 pimento-filled green olives
crackers of your choice to serve

Bring all the cheeses to room temperature. Use an electric mixer to combine all ingredients into a smooth pale orange mixture. The mix will be soft, so form into a larger teardrop-shaped ball for the abdomen and a smaller round ball for the head. Make sure your body shapes are large enough for the size crab legs you find, then wrap each in plastic wrap, adjust and smooth the shapes, and refrigerate at least overnight until solid.

Next, pat 8 cooked crab legs still in shells completely dry, then paint them with black food coloring using a brush. You might need a couple coats since once one layer of food coloring has dried, the next layer will stick better. We tried using food coloring spray but it did not cover enough. You may need an hour for the food coloring to dry enough to handle, so set aside until just before assembling. If you plan to eat the crab later, be sure to refrigerate the crab legs as the food coloring is drying.

After the cheese has set solid in the fridge, unpeel the plastic wrap and set it on your work surface. Sprinkle a good amount of black sesame seeds on the plastic wrap and carefully roll the cheese ball shape around so it is completely

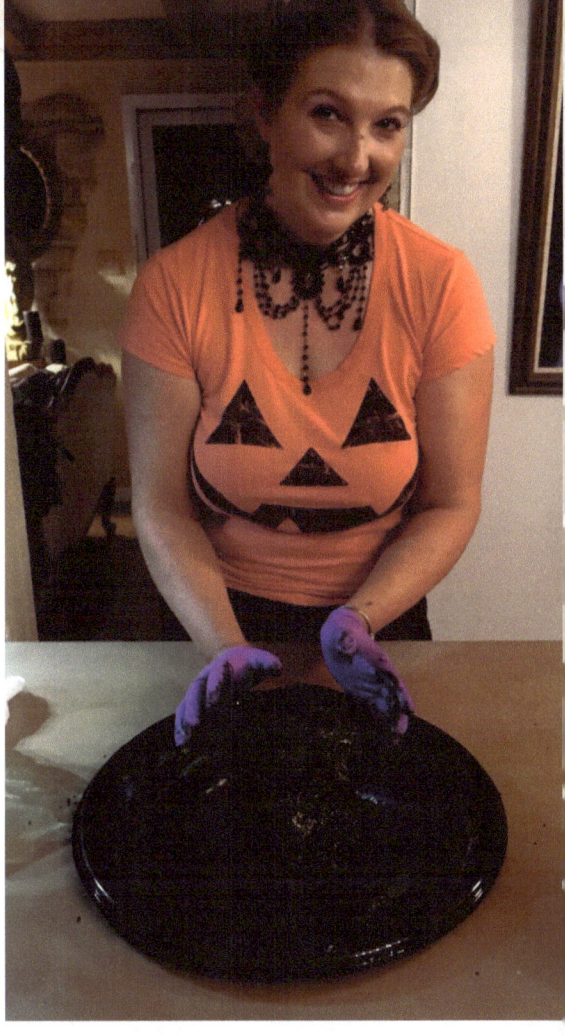

covered in black sesame seeds. Using the plastic wrap to help roll the cheese around helps prevent getting cheese on the outside of the sesame seeds from your cheesy fingers. Pat seeds into place to cover any cheese peeking through so the cheese ball is completely black. Place the seed-covered cheese balls on the serving plate in spider formation. Cut small indentations for the 8 olive eyeballs clustered in front like real spider eyes, then press the olives into place, pimento side staring outward. Add 4 black crab legs on each side under the abdomen closer to where the two cheese balls meet, arrange crackers on the plate to help keep the legs upright, then serve with a cheese knife stabbed in the side.

Food Safety Note: We bought cooked crab legs so there would be no cross-contamination concern of raw seafood, and we tucked the ends of the crab legs under the cheese ball so the majority of cheese never touched any crab. If your Gargantula is only out for a couple hours and not in hot conditions, you can probably enjoy eating the crab legs afterwards, but fair warning the black food coloring will start smearing and staining as soon as moisture hits it. Our Gargantula was at room temperature for over 8 hours, so we threw the crab legs away and only saved the cheese that never touched the crab, so that was about $10 wasted on presentation but worth it for the look! I did search for plastic crab legs but never found any full size that looked good enough to use. If you find some, please let me know!

# Savory Spiders with Gooey Guts

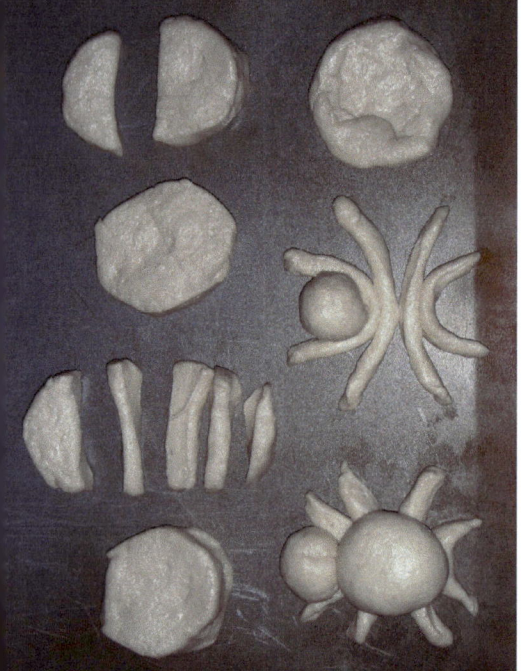

Yields 5 spiders.

1 package pop-open plain buttermilk biscuits
(not extra flaky, not cinnamon rolls)

**Vegetarian Gooey Guts**
nacho cheese sauce of your choice

**Carnivore Gooey Guts**
your favorite crumbled pre-cooked sausage
mixed with cheese sauce
or use your favorite sausage roll filling recipe

Preheat oven to 400° F per the package instructions. Use an ungreased non-stick baking sheet. Each spider requires two pre-shaped biscuits. Using clean kitchen shears, cut about 1/3rd of one biscuit away to be the head, then cut the remaining 2/3rds into 4 skinny strips for the legs. Twist the both ends of each strip to be pointy spider feet. Form the shortest strip it into a curved U-shape to be the back legs. Making sure they all touch, use the two the longer strips for the middle legs, then the other smaller strip curved into another U-shape for the front legs. All the legs should be touching each other in the middle underneath where the body will go. Take the other whole biscuit and tuck all the edges in to make a smooth ball. Place the tucked edges side down making firm contact on top the legs. Take the 1/3rd biscuit, tuck the edges in for a smooth ball for the head, then place the head in front touching the body.

If you want your spiders to have Gooey Guts, you can add the guts inside the body and head when you are tucking in the edges before assembling the spider. Put the cheese sauce into a baggie and cut one corner to make a piping hole. Shape the whole biscuit so it is curved and almost closed into a ball, then pipe the cheese sauce into the biscuit and seal the last edges around the cheese. Place the biscuit seam side down onto the legs. Usually the head is too small to fit cheese inside without making a giant mess, but you are welcome to try!

Bake the spider biscuits no more than 6 minutes at 400° F or the legs will burn. Your spiders will be barely golden brown but tasty, fluffy and tender.

# SOURDOUGH SPIDERS

I had made the Savory Spiders with Gooey Guts many years ago, but the purchased canned biscuit dough always puffed more than the elegant pointy black widow feet I wanted to see in my spiders...so I made Sourdough Spiders instead! These can be parbaked and frozen for reheating on party day, and they can even be kept in airtight metal tins for up to 2 days, but no longer or they could break your teeth!

Yield: about 3 dozen spiders

1 1/2 cups sourdough starter, recently fed
2 tablespoons sugar
1 teaspoon salt
3 tablespoons canola oil
1 egg, beaten (or equivalent vegan egg replacer)
2 cups all-purpose flour
gluten flour
(replace 1 Tbsp of gluten flour for each cup of all-purpose flour to hold shape better)

Feed sourdough starter overnight. In a large bowl add 1 1/2 cups of the fed sourdough starter, sugar, salt, oil, egg, 1 cup of flour, and gluten flour if desired. Stir together with a wooden spoon or beat with an electric mixer until the dough is shiny and elastic, 3 to 5 minutes. Add the remaining 1 cup flour and mix until incorporated. Turn the dough out onto a lightly floured work surface, cover with an inverted bowl and let stand for 15 minutes. On the lightly floured work surface, knead the dough until smooth and springy, 5 to 10 minutes. Place the dough in a large bowl, cover with plastic wrap and let rise until puffy, about 45 minutes.

If using a bread machine, spoon in 1 1/2 cups of the fed sourdough starter, then add the rest of ingredients and start the dough-only cycle for the machine to combine and knead the dough for you and rise in the warmth of the machine.

After the dough has risen, remove from machine and form into spider shapes on ungreased non-stick baking sheets. Portion the dough into thirds, then each third into twelve balls, but keep all the dough moist under a towel until ready to form into a spider. Split one ball in half, and roll one half into a smaller ball as the large abdomen. Split the other half into 4 long ropes plus a smaller ball for the head. Twist the both ends of each rope to be pointy spider feet. Form the shortest strip into a curved U-shape to be the back legs. Use the two longer ropes for the middle legs, then the other smaller rope curved into another U-shape for the front legs. All the legs should be touching each other in the middle underneath where the body will go. Place the large

**TRICKS & TIPS**
These can be made vegan, but using gluten flour to replace 1 tablespoon per cup of all-purpose flour holds the shape much better, so they are far from gluten-free.

abdomen ball where all the legs meet, making firm contact on top the legs. Take the last piece and roll into a smooth ball for the head, then place the head in front touching the body. If your dough is drying too much, moisten the contact points with water so the dough will stick together, otherwise pieces may pull apart while baking. Repeat until you have a baking sheet full to bake, then continue forming the rest of the dough into spiders.

Bake at 350F for 10 minutes or until done without burning the pointed feet. To freeze for later use, bake only about 4 minutes, just long enough to set the shape but still pale and soft inside, then freeze when cooled and store in zip-lock freezer bags. When ready to serve, bake until golden and crisp, about 5-10 minutes from frozen, shorter time if they are thawed to room temperature. These will have a crispy crust with only slight browning, so your spiders will be quite pale. You can add food coloring or sprinkle black sesame seeds on top before baking if you would like to add some darkness to your Sourdough Spiders.

## BONE BREADSTICKS

Bones and skeletons are perfectly spooky for Halloween, but how to make them tasty to eat? For sweet crunchy bones you can make my meringue Brittle Bones, but for savory sticks to dip into various sauces, try some Bone Breadsticks. There is a popular non-stick bone baking pan available, but using that for my sourdough breadsticks makes them pretty large and more chewy than crispy, so instead you can try the classic method of making smaller bone shapes by forming by hand and snipping the ends with kitchen shears. I have also had success with two other non-sourdough normal yeast recipes, so here are three different non-dairy vegan recipes for Bone Breadsticks!

# SOURDOUGH BONE BREADSTICKS

**Yield: about 3 dozen breadsticks**

2 teaspoons (one 1/4 ounce packet) active dry yeast (optional)
10 tablespoons warm water
1/2 cup sourdough starter, recently fed
2 teaspoons sugar
4 teaspoons veg oil
1 teaspoon salt
1/4 teaspoon soda
3 cups flour

Feed sourdough starter overnight. In a large bowl, combine the yeast, sugar and 1 cup lukewarm water (105 degrees to 115 degrees ). Let stand for 5 minutes until bubbly. Stir 1/2 cup of the fed sourdough starter, 2 cups of flour, and the rest of the ingredients into the yeast mixture. Stir together with a wooden spoon or beat with an electric mixer until the dough is shiny and elastic, 3 to 5 minutes. Add the remaining 1 cup flour and mix until incorporated. Turn the dough out onto a lightly floured work surface, cover with an inverted bowl and let stand for 15 minutes. On the lightly floured work surface, knead the dough until smooth and springy, 5 to 10 minutes. Place the dough in a large bowl, cover with plastic wrap and let rise until puffy, about 45 minutes.

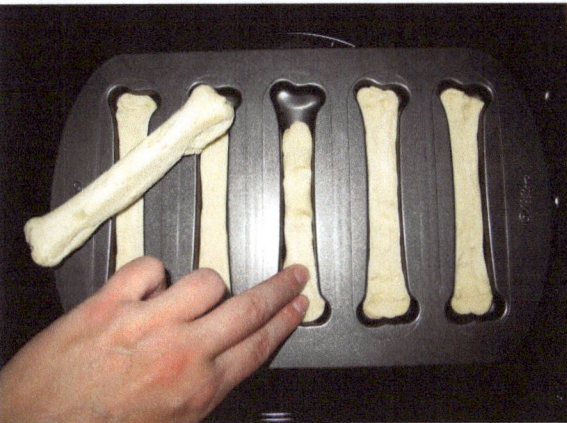

If using a bread machine, spoon 1/2 cup of the fed sourdough starter along with dry yeast and warm water, then add the rest of ingredients and start the dough-only cycle for the machine to combine and knead the dough for you and rise in the warmth of the machine. If your sourdough is vigorous, the active dry yeast is not necessary, but you still need the water for the dough to form the right texture.

After dough has risen, remove from machine and form into breadsticks. Press into a non-stick bone-shape baking pan, or form by hand, cutting strips, rolling them smooth, then cutting the end of the strips in half to make the joint ends. Bake at 350F for 10 minutes or until done. To freeze for later use, do not drizzle with olive oil and bake just long enough to set the shape but still pale and soft inside, then freeze when cooled. When ready to serve, bake until golden and crisp, about 30 minutes from frozen, shorter time if they are thawed to room temperature. These will have a crispy crust but pale colored instead of browning, perfect for bones!

# CRUNCHY BONE BREADSTICKS

**Yield: about 3 dozen breadsticks**

**2 teaspoons (one 1/4 ounce packet) active dry yeast**
**1 teaspoon sugar**
**2 1/2 cups flour**
**2 tablespoons extra-virgin olive oil**
**1 teaspoon table salt**

In a large bowl, combine the yeast, sugar and 1 cup lukewarm water (105 degrees to 115 degrees). Let stand for 5 minutes until bubbly. Stir 1 1/2 cups flour, 2 tablespoons olive oil and the table salt into the yeast mixture. Stir together with a wooden spoon or beat with an electric mixer until the dough is shiny and elastic, 3 to 5 minutes. Add the remaining 1 cup flour and mix until incorporated. Turn the dough out onto a lightly floured work surface, cover with an inverted bowl and let stand for 15 minutes. On the lightly floured work surface, knead the dough until smooth and springy, 5 to 10 minutes. Place the dough in a large bowl, cover with plastic wrap and let rise until puffy, about 45 minutes.

If using a bread machine, combine the yeast, sugar and 1 cup lukewarm water (105F degrees to 115F degrees ) in the bread machine. Let stand for 5 minutes until bubbly. Then add 2 Tbsp olive oil and the table salt into the yeast mixture, then add 2 1/2 cups flour. Set for the dough only cycle, and let rise about an hour after the cycle is complete.

Preheat the oven to 350F degrees. Drizzle olive oil over 2 baking sheets if desired, or use parchment paper or silicone mats. Divide the dough into sections, then roll and stretch small finger size bones until the baking sheet is full. After the pan is full, use kitchen shears to snip the ends of each bone and spread out the cut ends to make a bone shape. These really puff up so leave enough clearance between them. Bake until golden and crisp, about 30 minutes. Remove them from the oven, and cool on a rack.

Transfer the baking sheets to a rack and let the breadsticks cool completely. To freeze for later use, do not drizzle with olive oil and bake just long enough to set the shape but still pale and soft inside, then freeze when cooled. When ready to serve, bake until golden and crisp, about 30 minutes from frozen, shorter time if they are thawed to room temperature. Arrange your Crunchy Bone Breadsticks in a pile or a dismantled skeleton shape near a variety of dipping sauces for your guests to enjoy!

# THIN BONE BREADSTICKS

**Yield: about 3 dozen breadsticks**

2 teaspoons (one 1/4 ounce packet) active dry yeast
2 teaspoons sugar
1 1/4 teaspoons salt
3 cups (11 ounces) all-purpose flour
3/4 cup (6 ounces) lukewarm water
2 tablespoons (7/8 ounce) olive oil

Mix and knead the dough ingredients by hand, mixer, or bread machine set on the dough cycle to make a soft, supple dough. Divide the dough in half, cover with lightly greased plastic wrap, and let it rest and relax for at least 15 minutes up to an hour.

Preheat the oven to 425F. Drizzle olive oil over baking sheets if desired, or use parchment paper or silicone mats. Divide the dough into sections, then roll and stretch small finger size bones until the baking sheet is full. After the pan is full, use kitchen shears to snip the ends of each bone and spread out the cut ends to make a bone shape. Cover the breadsticks and let them rest and rise for 30 to 60 minutes, until they've puffed noticeably. Bake the breadsticks for 12 to 14 minutes, or until they're golden brown. Remove them from the oven, and cool on a rack.

To freeze for later use, do not drizzle with olive oil and bake just long enough to set the shape but still pale and soft inside, then freeze when cooled. When ready to serve, bake until golden and crisp, about 30 minutes from frozen, shorter time if they are thawed to room temperature. Arrange your Thin Crunchy Bone Breadsticks on a tray or standing in an urn near a variety of dipping sauces for your guests to enjoy!

# SOURDOUGH SKELETON

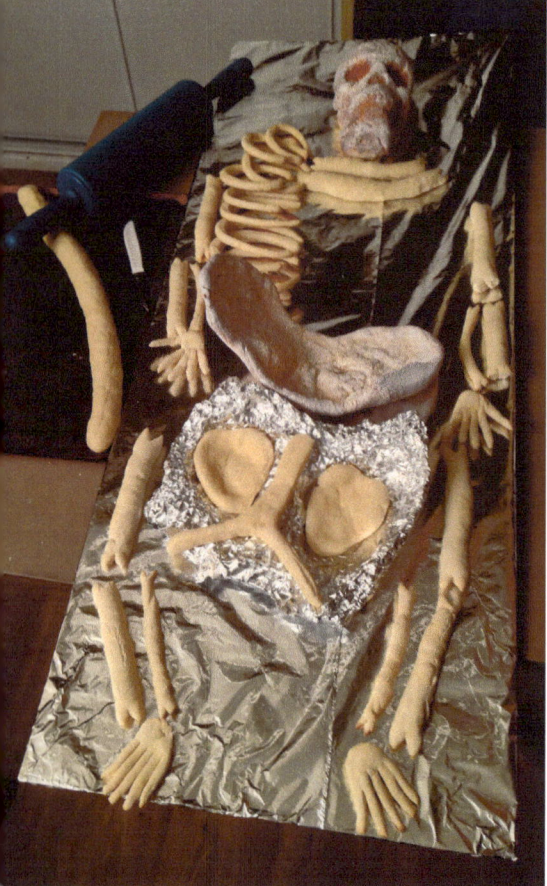

I wanted a large food display for my Day of the Dead party, so I used my Sourdough Bone Breadstick recipe to create an entire 5-foot-long Sourdough Skeleton! Many skeleton decorations for Dia de los Muertos are handcrafted in a more rustic style, which was a more forgiving design when you're not always sure how shapes will mutate and puff during baking.

I used my Sourdough Bone Breadstick recipe in a non-stick life-size skull baking pan for the head, which set the scale for the rest of the skeleton, but I hand-sculpted all the rest of the bone shapes, using foil supports while baking to keep curves intact, like for the collarbones, shoulder blades, and especially the hips. I used a smaller rubber skeleton as a model and created simpler shapes, like the entire spine as one curved shape with notches cut as vertebrae seams, and feet and hands like mittens so they could be posed more easily. I baked flat horseshoe shapes for the ribs, then angled them in display so they looked like they were bending around and connecting to the spine.

Due to all the different rounds of baking in the oven and different size pieces, it was difficult to control all the browning to match, so after everything was baked, I lightly brushed all the bones with opaque white food paint, leaving the eye sockets and teeth darker. That gave the Sourdough Skeleton a much more spooky look since it looked more like a Dia de los Muertos craft project than tasty bread!

I displayed the Sourdough Skeleton on a bed of lettuce leaves over a foil-covered cardboard scrap. The full leaves made it a little tricky to pose the bones properly, so shredded lettuce or more flexible leaves might work better. I set out bowls of Bone Breadsticks for party guests to eat to leave the skeleton for everyone to appreciate, and the Violent Vertebrae made it a whole table of bones!

# Dia de los Muertos Delights

The family-centered, brightly-colorful, and creatively creepy Mexican holiday of Dia de los Muertos "Day of the Dead" has become even more well-known outside of Mexico in recent years, with many Halloween stores selling costumes, face tattoos, decorations, servingware, and even edible art supplies, like elaborate cookie sugar skull style cookie cutters that imprint designs into the dough. My Eerie Elegance Scream Team now includes Scary Jerry, our resident expert on Dia de los Muertos through his own Mexican family traditions, so we hosted an entire Day of the Dead Halloween party in 2015, complete with a special new menu inspired by authentic recipes!

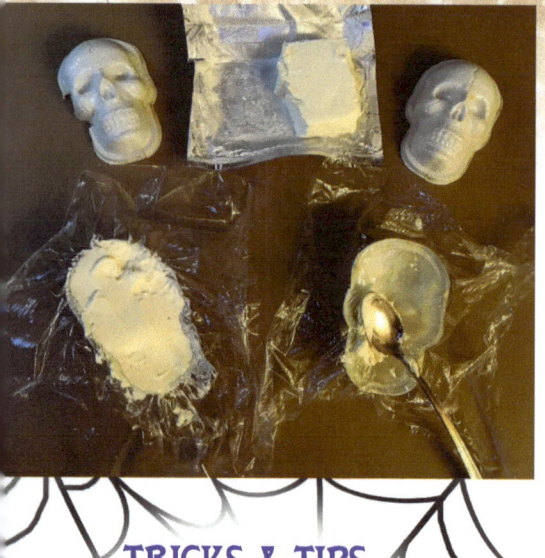

# SINISTER SKULLS CREAM CHEESE CALAVERAS

I've made my molded cream cheese Sinister Skulls for over 20 years now, but for my Day of the Dead Halloween party, I updated them sugar-skull-style as Cream Cheese Calaveras!

**plastic wrap**
**1 small skull mold**
**1 package cream cheese**
**1 jar chili sauce or salsa**
**crackers for spreading**

This is more edible art than a full recipe since the only ingredients are softened cream cheese and food coloring with piping bags and tips, but you will need a skull mold for these. Over twenty years ago I found small plastic skull candy cups that I've used almost every year for Sinister Skulls, carefully nursing them along as they've gotten brittle and started cracking, but now you can find all sorts of skull shaped pans and molds in several sizes online and in specialty food and craft stores.

Line your mold with plastic wrap first, since no matter how non-stick, your cream cheese will NOT come out from the mold easily! Spoon softened cream cheese into the mold, pressing firmly to force cream cheese into all the crevices. Fold the plastic wrap over the top so the cheese doesn't dry out, then place in the fridge to chill to set the shape. If you have limited molds and want to make more skulls, after the skull shape is set, remove the skull keeping it sealed in the plastic wrap, then gently wrap it in foil to cushion the face shape. They will stay a few weeks fine in the fridge, and you can freeze them for a few days, but freezing them too long causes the cheese to crumble after it thaws.

There you already have the original Sinister Skulls version ready to serve, but to take it up a notch, add food coloring of your choice to thawed cream cheese and fill piping bags with each color. You can also paint food coloring directly on the cream cheese as long as you use a very gentle touch with a pliable watercolor brush. Do not bother with food coloring pens since they just carve into the cream cheese. Decorate the skulls with scrolls, flowers, hearts, dots, even gold and other edible pearls or candy quins as your imagination is inspired by Dia de los Muertos decor.

To serve, place the skull in a shallow dish, garnish with your preferred bloody salsa or chili mixture, including inside the eye sockets if they aren't already decorated, and stab with your favorite spreader ready for nearby crackers.

## TRICKS & TIPS

You can extend the time before needing to refill by placing the skull on half a block of cream cheese, but cover the plain cream cheese with enough sauce so you can only see the skull above the "blood."

# CHILI LIME CORN CUPS

A favorite street food in Mexico is corn on the cob slathered with chili and lime. That form factor is a bit too large for a finger-food buffet feeding more than 50 guests, so I turned the corncob idea into a tortilla cup appetizer that is just as tasty but not too spicy. Butter gives even more flavor, but if you only use oil instead, your Chili Lime Corn Cups will be dairy-free and vegan.

**for roasting corn kernels:**

8 oz frozen corn kernels
3 Tbsp olive oil to roast corn kernels
kosher salt
freshly ground black pepper

**for final mixture:**

8 oz roasted corn kernels (see above)
8 Tbsp olive oil
2 teaspoons chili powder
1/4 teaspoon chipotle powder, or 1/4 teaspoon adobo sauce (from a can of chipotle peppers en adobo)
zest of 1 lime (approximately 2 tsp)
juice of 1 lime (approximately 2 tsp)
1 small red onion, finely chopped (optional)
1 orange or red pepper, chopped
15 oz can of black beans, rinsed and drained

If you're not lucky enough to find already-roasted frozen corn kernels like me, start by roasting your frozen corn kernels to add flavor. Heat broiler to low. Toss frozen corn kernels with 3 Tbsp olive oil, spread kernels onto a baking sheet, and sprinkle with salt and pepper. Roast 6-8 minutes until corn just starts turning brown. Set aside to cool.

Combine olive oil, chili powder, chipotle powder or adobo sauce, the zest of one lime, and the juice of one lime in a bowl until mixed. Add the chopped pepper, cooled roasted corn kernels, rinsed and drained black beans, and chopped onion if you like. Toss to coat all the corn kernels, then spread onto a baking sheet to roast again under broiler set to low for 5-10 minutes. Season with salt and pepper to taste.

The corn kernel mixture can be made in advance and frozen, but reheat in the oven to thaw, then let cool and spoon the mixture into tortilla chip cups for serving at room temperature for your guests to enjoy one of the flavors of Mexico in an no-mess bite!

# QUESO FUNDIDO

You can never go wrong with a melted cheese dip, especially with mushrooms and an extra Mexican-inspired kick from chipotles! Keep this fondue-like dip warm in a crockpot during your party, perfect for dipping Bone Breadsticks from your Sourdough Skeleton, or with strong tortilla chips or crackers.

**6 cups sliced crimini mushrooms, white button mushrooms, or ever fuller-flavor mushrooms like oyster or shiitake**
**3 chipotles chiles en adobo, seeded and thinly sliced**
**1 sliced medium red onion (optional)**
**1 1/2 Tbsp olive oil**
**32 oz grated sharp cheddar cheese**
**32 oz grated mozzarella**
**16 oz grated pepper jack cheese**
**1/4 tsp salt**
**black pepper to taste**

Start warming your crockpot while you saute the mushrooms. In a large non-stick skillet, heat the oil over medium-high. Add the sliced onion if desired, and cook, stirring frequently, until softening and beginning to brown, about 5 minutes. Add the mushrooms and stir nearly constantly until they have softened and any juice they release has evaporated, about 5 minutes longer. Stir in the sliced chiles, then taste and season with salt, usually about 1/4 teaspoon.

Transfer the hot mushroom mixture into your already-warm crockpot, and immediately add all the grated cheese, stirring to melt the cheese into the mushrooms until you have a creamy cheesy dip. Making this ahead will not reheat very well so prepare immediately before serving. Keep the crockpot on the lowest heat setting while serving, stirring periodically or it might get clumpy, but that didn't stop my guests from enjoying it!

# SAVORY SKULL PIZZAS

I usually have Halloween parties with enough guests that a buffet menu is easier to manage, but if you're having a smaller party with a grill or oven available, you could serve some Savory Skull Pizzas! You can imprint the eyes, nose and teeth into each skull-shaped personal-size crust, and get creative with pizza toppings so every guest can design their favorite pizza. Pepperoni or sliced olives work great for eyeballs, and cut cheese slices smaller as teeth!

To prepare for grilling pizza, bake your individual crust shapes only 2 minutes each side at 350F just to set the shape. When cooled, if keeping 2 days or more, freeze them in large zip bags with waxed paper between crusts to prevent sticking, then thaw completely for a couple hours before grilling.

Since the heat comes mostly from under the grill, give a quick spray of olive oil on both sides of the crust and place it on the grill top down for some crunch, remove from the grill to add toppings, then back onto the grill right-side up with the grill cover on for thorough heating of the toppings. This prevents the toppings from making the top crust soggy. For oven-baked pizzas, the top-down step isn't necessary since the heat is more even.

## WHOLE WHEAT SOURDOUGH PIZZA DOUGH

1 1/2 cup already-fed sourdough starter
2/3 cup water
1 1/2 tsp sugar
1 tsp salt
3 cups white whole wheat flour (can be all-purpose or bread flour)
2 1/4 tsp (1 packet) active dry yeast

Feed sourdough starter with 1 cup warm water and 1 cup all-purpose flour. Use 1 1/2 cups for the recipe and reserve the rest as new starter. Put ingredients into a bread machine in order with yeast on top and run the dough-only cycle. When dough is ready, shape into 9 individual pizza crusts approximately 6 inches in diameter, in any shape you like. Bake the individual crust shapes only 2 minutes each side at 350F just to set the shape. After cooling, store them in large zip bags with waxed paper between crusts to prevent sticking. If keeping 2 days or more, freeze the bags, then thaw completely for a couple hours before grilling. For oven-baked pizzas, thawing is not required.

### TRICKS & TIPS
You can also buy pizza dough at many grocery stores now, then you can portion into individual crust sizes and form them into skull shapes.

# PEQUEÑO PAN DE MUERTOS

Pan de Muertos is a round loaf of slightly-sweet, orange essence bread topped with an abstract skull and crossbones design and a sugar glaze. It is traditionally served for Dia de los Muertos family celebrations, offered and displayed on ancestors' gravestones and altar ofrendas to be enjoyed by the dead as well as the living. It takes time to form the skull and crossbones design so small, and since the dough keeps rising as you are forming the shapes, work quickly or they might distort the shape too much before baking. You can find several versions of the traditional full size bread recipe online, but those are too dense for small rolls, so I added orange extract to a vegan dinner roll recipe to make these small "pequeño" Pan de Muertos.

**1 packet (1 Tbsp) dry yeast**
**1/4 cup warm water (110F)**

**2 3/4 cup all-purpose flour**
**1/4 cup granulated sugar**
**3/4 tsp salt**
**1 tsp orange extract**
**1/2 cup warm water**
**1/4 cup oil**
**1 egg (or equivalent amount of vegan egg replacer)**
**granulated sugar for sprinkling**

Dissolve yeast in 1/4 cup warm water, then add rest of ingredients. Blend in a food processor or stir by hand until the dough forms a ball. Knead 10 minutes. Place in warm, greased bowl, cover with a towel, and place in warm spot to rise until doubled (about 1 to 1 1/2 hours). Punch down.

If using a bread machine, dissolve the yeast in 1/4 cup warm water in a small bowl. Add the other ingredients to the machine in the order listed above, add the dissolved yeast last, then use the dough-only cycle.

Prepare baking sheets with parchment paper. Divide kneaded dough into 3 portions. Divide each portion into 12 small balls, and pinch enough off each ball for 3 thin crossing ropes and a tiny ball on top where the ropes cross, as pictured. Let the first tray of finished mini-loaves rise under a towel until doubled in size, hopefully once you have finished forming the second tray. Bake the first tray while the second tray rises until doubled. Bake each tray at 350F for 5 minutes, sprinkle granulated sugar on top, the continue baking until golden brown, watching carefully so the sugar does not burn. Cool on rack, then store in zip bags up to 2 days to keep soft until serving. Makes about 36 mini rolls as Pequeño Pan de Muertos.

# CHAMPURRADO CHOCOLATE

Traditional champurrado is Mexican hot chocolate thickened with corn flour masa. For my Day of the Dead theme, instead of drinking chocolate, I adjusted this recipe to be a non-dairy fudge sauce, thick enough to be a perfect dip for the Bone Breadsticks, still smooth at room temperature because of the honey. You can serve the sauce warm in a small one quart crockpot, but keep stirring if it thickens or clumps over time.

1 tsp cinnamon
1/2 cup chopped Mexican chocolate (3 pucks)
1/2 cup water - bring to a simmer
1/2 cup corn flour w 1/2 cup water mixed smooth
1/2 cup honey

Bring cinnamon, chopped Mexican chocolate and water to a simmer in a pot, stirring constantly until chocolate melts. In a separate bowl, mix the corn dough with a cup of water until smooth. Pour the corn mixture into the hot chocolate, stirring constantly. Add the honey to the pot and stir until you have a smooth sauce, perfect for dipping.

### TRICKS & TIPS

For drinking chocolate like traditional champurrado, add 4-5 cups milk and stir while simmering until the milk has thickened so the mixture is the consistency of heavy cream.

# CREATIVE CALAVERA COOKIES

Decorating your own cookie is a fun party activity for children and adults alike, so instead of decorating a full sugar skull calavera with glue and trinkets like traditional calaveras, why not decorate your own Creative Calavera Cookie, perhaps even as a contest for everyone to vote which skull decor they like best?

Our cookie decorating station was a whole brightly-lit table in front of a shelf rack against the wall to display the final cookies, with small cards for each entrant to write their name by their cookie. Royal icing works best because once it sets for a few minutes it will dry hard, but you will need to mix that yourself and portion it into colors for piping bags or small refillable decorating tubes. Small purchased frosting tubes usually never dry so will drip and cannot stack, but they are an easy way to supply various colors. Our Creative Calavera Cookies Contest announced, "Use anything on this table to decorate your own cookie and you may win a prize!" We set out gold and other edible pearls, colorful candy quins in stars and diamond shapes, food coloring pens, and various colors of icing in small tubes so guests could have fun creating! Traditional sugar skull designs include scrolls, flowers, hearts, dots, even gold, jewels and lace, so it is helpful to provide some Dia de los Muertos sugar skull designs nearby as inspiration. Be prepared for a big mess so you might want to use a disposable tablecloth!

Scary Jerry already owned these fun sugar skull cookie stamps, but since the chin was too rounded to stand on the display shelf, I bent my own skull-shaped outside cookie cutter from copper pipe strapping and metal tape. My Foolproof Sugar Cookie recipe works perfectly for these since it doesn't spread, so the stamp design stays visible and the cookie keeps its outer shape. I did not use a basecoat of royal icing for these cookies since that would cover the stamp designs, and I thought the pale cookie color looked enough like bone. If you do not use a cookie stamp, you can use bright white royal icing in advance for a nice smooth basecoat.

# DIA DE LOS S'MUERTOS

**chocolate skulls, decoration optional**
**marshmallows**
**graham cracker squares**

Hosting Halloween for so many years now, I have acquired many baking and candy tools, including adorable silicone ice cube trays in perfect little skull shapes. Melting chocolate chips and pouring into these molds makes a perfect size chocolate chunk for sitting in a s'more with graham crackers and marshmallows, and how could I resist such a clever caption as Dia de los S'Muertos? Even just basic chocolate you already have skull s'mores! For bonus points, you can find edible opaque white food paints suitable for painting on chocolate available for sale online, and I love how my fine painted calavera-style designs looked on the finished s'mores! You could also use white candy melts for white chocolate skulls, but food coloring pens don't like sticking to the waxy surface of chocolate, so you'd need to tint some chocolate paint first.

My experience is that decorating each skull will take you a while, so keep the rest of the chocolate skulls in the refrigerator, and touch the skulls as little as possible so they do not melt under the warmth of your fingers. These look best as open-faced s'mores so you can see the skulls, especially if they are decorated! I set up all my s'mores on a tray since everyone was going to roast their own, but you could torch the marshmallows on the graham crackers first, then set the skulls on top if there's no roasting fire at your event.

### TRICKS & TIPS
Store your finished skulls in the refrigerator until serving, but do not freeze chocolate.

# Gingerbread Goodies

# GINGER WEB COOKIES

Autumn is the beginning of spice season, so gingerbread cookies are perfect for Halloween! For my Victorian spider-themed menu, I thought Ginger Web Cookies was a clever rhyme to the Gingerbread Cookies authentic from Victorian times, but updated to be vegan for my party guests.

**Yields about 5 dozen small web-shaped cookies**

1/2 cup butter (or non-dairy baking margarine)
1/2 cup molasses
1/2 cup brown sugar
1 tablespoon ginger
1 tablespoon cinnamon
1 scant teaspoon allspice
1 scant teaspoon cloves
2 teaspoon baking soda
1 egg (or vegan egg replacer)
2 1/2 cups flour

Soften the butter in the bowl. In a separate bowl, stir the spices into the brown sugar, then add to the butter and mix until creamy. Add the egg, molasses and baking soda and mix thoroughly. Add flour, then chill until set. Transfer sheet of dough to baking sheet or roll directly on a silicone baking mat before cutting to avoid distorting final cookie shape. Roll dough to 1/8" thick, cut with web-shape cutter and remove extra dough to re-roll. Bake at 350 degrees F for about 5 minutes or until barely firm but not browned. Let cool on a baking rack while you mix white royal icing. After cookies are completely cool, pipe the web designs with white royal icing using a thin writing tip. After the white webs are dry, you can pipe black spiders sitting on the webs, like the royal icing Spooky Spiders. Let the royal icing dry overnight before stacking any cookies. Your Ginger Web Cookies will keep at least two weeks in an airtight tin.

# GINGERBREAD GARGOYLES

It's amazing what you can find on the Internet these days! While browsing cookie cutters, I happened across this giant gargoyle copper cookie cutter, so I splurged. You can also make your own cookie cutters from online kits, or you can be adventurous at the hardware store finding your own supplies. Avoid galvanized metals, but clean copper is food safe as long as you wash it well. This recipe is just as tasty with vegan substitutions. I have other sugar cookies on my menu, so I thought some Gingerbread Gargoyles would be good variety without requiring too much final decoration.

Yields about 15 1/8th-inch thick large gargoyles

Mix the same gingerbread cookie dough as the Ginger Web Cookies, then chill until set. Roll thick enough for intricate shapes like gargoyles to stay intact, at least 1/8th inch or thicker. Transfer sheet of dough to baking sheet before cutting to avoid distorting final cookie shape. Bake at 350 degrees F for about 5 minutes or until barely firm but not browned. Baking time will be longer for thicker cookies. Decorate with colored royal icing after cookies are completely cooled. Now your castle keep will be protected by Gingerbread Gargoyles, at least until they are gobbled up by guests!

## TRICKS & TIPS
Spot the 13 Spooky Storieis shown by the creepy clues and characters in and around the Ghoulish Gingerbread Haunted House! Answers at the end!

# GHOULISH GINGERBREAD HAUNTED HOUSE

Fair warning that this massive project took me two years of failed attempts until the third try was the charm! A gingerbread project of this size with this much detail is highly ambitious, but you might enjoy learning various techniques that might inspire you for other edible art projects.

Way back in 1999 after I made my gingerbread thatched cottage in the summer, I thought it would be fun to make a gingerbread haunted house for Halloween, complete with fun tiny details. That very same fall a famous decorating magazine was selling a big fancy kit for a gingerbread haunted house, so I decided against it that year. As my parties got more elaborate, the idea kept getting postponed, until I was able to do my lighted gingerbread castle in 2007. It was just as well that I waited so long because I have learned so many more cool edible art techniques over the years that the end result was much better.

I also designed this gingerbread house big enough to scratch some of my dollhouse miniatures itch that had been unsatisfied for years, plus I was even able to make it into a quiz activity for my party guests! You too can play the quiz as you read here by spotting the 13 spooky stories shown by the creepy clues and characters in and around the haunted house. I'll reveal the answers at the very end after showing the three-year saga of creating my Giant Ghoulish Gingerbread Haunted House and its ultimate demise!

## GINGERBREAD DESIGN

Before you start any edible work, first you need a design. You can use my pattern template to make a smaller scale but still spooky gingerbread haunted house by downloading the resizable template from my website, enlarging everything together to the size you like, then printing and cutting the pieces.
http://www.EerieElegance.com/GingerbreadTemplate.html

Of course you can always design your own! Scrap corrugated cardboard boxes work well for gingerbread mockups since you need to account for the thickness of the gingerbread for how pieces fit together, and the corrugation is about the same thickness you should roll gingerbread dough for walls. I had quite a mess of cutting and taping before I had my design, then I labeled everything and carefully cut through tape so I could use the cardboard as template pieces to bake the gingerbread. Do not create your mockup so large that you have no cookie sheets or oven space to bake large gingerbread walls!

## SCULPTING EDIBLE ART CHARACTERS & ACCESSORIES

I sculpted the character figures from gum paste, modeling chocolate, fondant and royal icing, handpainting with food coloring and food pens for final details, and rice cereal treats to shape the hand hedge. My marshmallow fondant jack o'lanterns were sculpted to fit over battery tealights so they would flicker along the walkway to the front porch. To hide the tealights under the pumpkins, I spread green royal icing directly on the sides of the battery tealights and dipped them in cookie crumb dirt, which worked really well! Royal icing snaps off of non-porous surfaces so I cleaned the tealights fine later.

All the characters were sculpted and decorated as much as possible well before final placement in and around the haunted house. As long as you have sanitary plastic bins to protect against possible critters and silica gel packets to keep any extra moisture under control, sculptures made from gum paste, fondant, royal icing, and modeling chocolate can all last a few years. Sugar work and cotton candy is trickier since they're much more sensitive to air moisture which makes pulled, molded and spun sugar sticky, so save your sugar work until just before final display.

Gum paste holds fine detail extremely well, often used to make realistic edible flowers. It is the most moisture-tolerant and firmly rigid but very lightweight when dry, and it is technically edible but doesn't taste like much. You can purchase gum paste at baking supply and craft stores either as powder you mix with water, or as premixed paste in airtight bags. You can mix food coloring into the gum paste as you are sculpting or paint afterwards since gum paste dries with a matte finish.

Modeling chocolate is much heavier so weight can be an issue, but it is much tastier. You can purchase premixed modeling chocolate in various colors in bulk online, but mixing up small batches of modeling chocolate at home is very useful, since it's just adding the right amount of light corn syrup to melted chocolate, and as long as it's gel food coloring, not the watery liquid kinds, you can make dark chocolate black or white chocolate any color you like. You need to be careful about the warmth of your hands when sculpting with modeling chocolate, so if it starts getting too sticky and floppy, leave it to cool down then come back to it later. It is more difficult to paint on modeling chocolate since it has a waxy surface, but often if you let the first coat of food coloring dry, the second coat will stick better. You can also purchase special white chocolate paints online that work great and can be tinted with gel food coloring.

## MODELING CHOCOLATE RECIPES

**Dark Chocolate Modeling Paste:**
7 ounces (200 grams) bittersweet chocolate, chopped
1/4 cup (60 ml) light corn syrup

**Semi-Sweet Chocolate Modeling Paste:**
7 ounces (200 grams) semi-sweet chocolate, chopped
3 1/2 - 4 tablespoons light corn syrup

**White Chocolate Modeling Paste:**
7 ounces (200 grams) white chocolate, chopped
1 1/2 - 2 tablespoons light corn syrup

**Milk Chocolate Modeling Paste:**
7 ounces (200 grams) milk chocolate
2 1/2 - 3 tablespoons light corn syrup

Melt the chocolate in the microwave on half-power 30 seconds at a time so it does not overheat or burn. Remove from microwave and stir until smooth and cooled a bit. Stir in the corn syrup. The chocolate will stiffen almost immediately. Stir until completely combined. Spread the chocolate mixture on plastic wrap on a baking sheet and cover with more plastic wrap, then refrigerate until firm (about two hours). When the dough is firm, remove from the refrigerator, and knead it until it is soft enough to work with. If it is too hard, cut off small pieces, and knead until pliable. If you do not have silicone mats, grease the counter where you are working with oil or non-stick spray so the chocolate won't stick. Sculpt the chocolate into any shape you like. Well wrapped in plastic inside zip bags it will keep for months. If it gets hard to work with, microwave about 20-30 seconds or knead in a little more corn syrup until it is pliable again.

### TRICKS & TIPS
To make black modeling cohcolate, start with dark chocolate so you don't use as much gel food coloring.

Store-bought cake fondant is usually vegan and sometimes kosher, but it is also quite expensive. If those dietary concerns are not an issue for your project, you can also make your own fondant cheaper and tastier using marshmallows and powdered sugar, but if you do not own a stand mixer and must knead by hand, it will be an extremely sticky, stringy mess before it forms a dough!

## MARSHMALLOW FONDANT

**16 ounces (1 bag) white mini marshmallows**
**2-5 tablespoons water**
**32 ounces (2 lbs) powdered confectioners' sugar**
**solid vegetable shortening to protect hands and equipment!**

Place the marshmallows and 2 tablespoons of water in a large bowl. Microwave 30 seconds on high, then stir until mixed well. Continue microwaving and stirring until melted, about 2 1/2 minutes total.

Place 3/4 of the confectioners' sugar on top of the melted marshmallow mixture. Fold sugar into marshmallow mixture. Flavoring can be added at this point if desired. Place solid vegetable shortening in easily accessed bowl so you can reach into it with fingers as you are working. Grease hands and counter GENEROUSLY; turn marshmallow mixture onto counter. Start kneading like you would dough. Continue kneading, adding additional confectioners' sugar and re-greasing hands and counter so the fondant doesn't stick. If the marshmallow fondant is tearing easily, it is too dry; add water (about 1/2 tablespoon at a time) kneading until fondant forms a firm, smooth elastic ball that will stretch without tearing, about 8 minutes. Tint with food coloring, kneading until your desired shade. This process is MUCH easier if you have a stand mixer with a dough hook, but be sure to grease everything with shortening extremely well!

Double-wrap the fondant in plastic and let rest overnight. When not actively working with the fondant, make sure to keep it covered with plastic wrap or in a bag to prevent it from drying out. When ready to use, knead fondant until smooth and roll or sculpt as desired.

## BAKING THE GINGERBREAD

If you are making a small gingerbread house, you can use the cookie recipe from earlier in this chapter, but for large projects like this I use structural gingerbread, which has no eggs and uses shortening as the fat so it never spoils and has much less chance of getting soggy. I don't use this for cookies since it's not as tender and crispy, but that's why it's much better for walls if you want them to stay standing!

## STRUCTURAL GINGERBREAD HOUSE RECIPE

1 cup shortening
1 cup sugar
1 cup molasses
Melt the above ingredients in a saucepan. Then add...
5 cups flour
1 teaspoon baking soda
1 teaspoon salt
1 teaspoon nutmeg
3 teaspoons ginger

Only use a mixer for first 4 cups, then knead until crumbly. If not using immediately, refrigerate dough then warm for 1 hour before rolling. If your dough is too dry, mist with water just enough to moisten. Dough may look crumbly at the edges when rolling, but the middle will compact into a dense sheet. Roll thick onto silicone mats or parchment, cut into shapes around your templates, then pull away the extra dough, so you do not distort your shapes. Bake for 15 minutes at 350F. Trim around your template again for each piece while the dough is still warm, since the shape expands slightly while cooking, and when cooled this gingerbread is rock hard. Assemble your gingerbread house with royal icing or melted sugar, and decorate as desired.

Roll your structural gingerbread dough onto silicone mats or parchment paper so you do not need to move the pieces before baking. Do not roll thinner than 1/8th inch, and larger walls may need to be thicker to be more stable. Cut around your templates, including windows and doors according to the design, paying attention to pieces that need multiple copies. To keep track of all the pieces, make a checklist or stack your matching cooled pieces together so you can count them easily. You can make your own larger cookie sheets using strong cardboard covered with foil, however structural gingerbread still has limits, and a large flat ceiling may sag under its own weight or crush the side walls. I had to use sections of foam core board for both my ceilings for this haunted house because the gingerbread I baked cracked in the middle, but the same shapes in a smaller size may be fine. Royal icing seams between smaller walls give more stability, along with corners and pointed roof pieces holding each other in place.

## DECORATING THE WALLS

You can decorate your house after assembly, but since I was decorating inside and out, I piped as much as possible on both sides of the walls before assembly, then touched up as needed. For the exterior, I piped flat planks of royal icing siding using a wide ribbon/rose tip. Not only did that give a finished look, but once the royal icing hardened, it helped keep the tall gingerbread walls

from sagging in ambient moisture. I needed 9 cups of pale lavender gray royal icing to hand-pipe all the exterior siding, then shaded them spookier with black and purple food coloring sprays. The siding had to dry completely before I could turn them over to decorate the inside walls, so they were out on the table overnight. I even piped railings and the large entry gate from melted black chocolate flat onto silicone mats, making spiderweb designs look like spiky wrought iron. I loved how they looked, but by the end of all that piping, my hand was pretty cramped!

After years of resisting temptation, I finally I invested in an edible printer mainly for the wallpaper design I had planned, but that led to other fun printables that ended up quite impressive and easier than hand-decorating, like the Tasty Tombstones in the graveyard, wood plank flooring, the Picture of Dorian Gray from the 1945 film, some Haunted Mansion portraits, fun vintage anatomy charts and the dartboard for the lab, and even a portrait of my steampunk character for the living room. I cut the wallpaper frosting sheets to the size of each wall including window cutouts, and attached to the gingerbread with a little spread of royal icing, sealing the edge with the top rail of the wainscoting, which was raw gingerbread behind brown royal icing handpiped planks. I printed the portraits separately, attached them with royal icing, then added frames and other 3D accents piped over the top, gilding them with luster dust after they were dry. I really love the huge bookcase, and extra cool that it's from a photo I took at Lord Byron's ancestral home in England!

## GINGERBREAD CONSTRUCTION

After setting the party tablecloth in place and adding plastic protection over it, I decided on the original large board on a turntable as the gingerbread house base, since it barely turned all the way around, had just enough yard space, and still left room for a couple plates on either side of the table. Everything had dried well overnight, so with Scary Jerry's help we had the two stories assembled in under three hours, with the roof & bay window waiting until the base stories were fully stable overnight.

I have seen melted sugar used as a stronger and faster seam for gingerbread construction, but I found it much more difficult to use with more dangerous mess, since the melted sugar is harder to control, and drips can burn skin immediately. I prefer using stiff royal icing in a piping bag, especially since you can tint it to match your gingerbread color exactly. You may need helping hands from a friend like Scary Jerry or lots of jars and other heavy objects to hold your royal icing in place as it sets enough to attach the next pieces. I also tried using meringue powder royal icing for all the house siding, but that royal icing ended up a more spongy texture, so I prefer using raw egg whites in the recipe provided earlier. Pasteurized egg whites in a carton works as well as cracking the eggs yourself, plus not so many yolks leftover.

### TRICKS & TIPS
I prefer using stiff royal icing in a piping bag for assembly, especially since you can tint it to match your gingerbread color exactly.

## COOKING, MOLDING, PULLING & SPINNING SUGAR

While waiting for the walls to set, I made the sugar glass for the lab glassware and crystal ball custom molds I had made, made the pulled sugar mess on the stove, and used the leftover hard candy to make the cotton candy mess outside to add later as the graveyard fog.

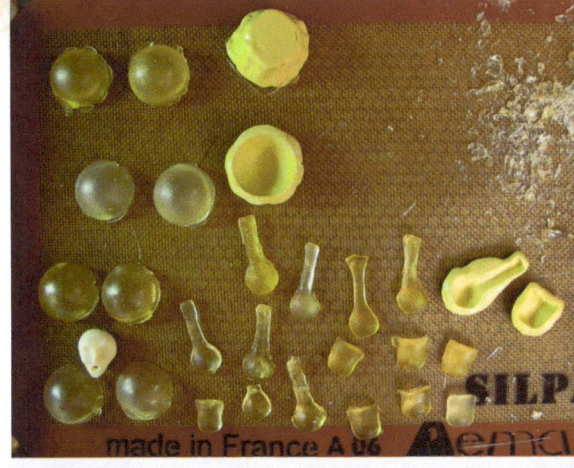

I had made a 2-part food-grade silicone mold of a ping pong ball, and sculpted Leota's head sized for the mold from white chocolate with royal icing hair, with features drawn with green food coloring pen to make her look ghostly. When I poured my

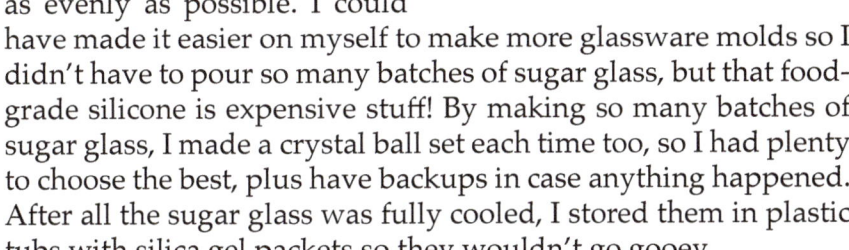

sugar glassware for the lab, also in smaller silicone molds I had made, I poured the crystal ball halves, making sure each mold was coated completely and evenly but then dumping the excess out right away so only a thin layer of sugar was in the mold. I set them open side down on the silicone mat to cool so they could drain & set as evenly as possible. I could have made it easier on myself to make more glassware molds so I didn't have to pour so many batches of sugar glass, but that food-grade silicone is expensive stuff! By making so many batches of sugar glass, I made a crystal ball set each time too, so I had plenty to choose the best, plus have backups in case anything happened. After all the sugar glass was fully cooled, I stored them in plastic tubs with silica gel packets so they wouldn't go gooey.

I had seen pulled sugar art on cooking shows but I hadn't had much practice myself, so I was glad my spooky trees were forgiving shapes! These two pulled sugar trees used the rest of a batch of sugar glass after filling the few molds. After the sugar cooled to taffy stage spread flat on a silicone mat, I used kitchen shears to cut branches from the top half keeping them attached to the bottom half, cutting smaller branches from the larger ones, twisted them into shape, then twisted the main trunk, letting the final shape cool in place leaning on the house and anything else the right size as supports to make the flat base. When the sugar was completely cool, I used brown icing to cover the sugar like bark, plus it helped protect the sugar from ambient moisture. The trees leaned in place on the house, and I think they turned out perfectly spooky.

## EDIBLE GLOW EFFECTS

I had saved placing the sugar glass for last because the weather was already getting more humid. I glued the sugar beakers and flasks in place with royal icing on the lab table holes so they would be lighted from underneath as the battery lights changed colors.

I was also so very pleased that Madame Leota's crystal ball worked so well! I chose the best crystal ball pieces, set Leota's head inside the back half, and I used an open flame very quickly to heat the seam so the two halves would stick together without discoloring the sugar.

It all stayed together resting in place on the hole in the table, and with the color-changing battery light hidden under the seance table, it looked even more magical than I had hoped!

## FINISHING THE FURNITURE & ACCESSORIES

I had thought I would assemble the furniture before piping, but then realized after the first couple were assembled that would be much more difficult, so everything was piped in flat pieces as a "carved" pattern first, then assembled after they were completely dry. To finish the furniture and accessories, I mixed some marshmallow fondant purple with the mixer, then rolled out all the purple fondant furniture cushions and tablecloth, draping it over the gingerbread seance table, making sure no light could peek through at the floor, then cut the top hole so it could dry enough overnight for surface decorating. I assembled the pipe organ & furniture using brown royal icing glue, the tower & main roof separately assembled on the table, and the bay window added to the house, so they could all dry overnight.

I struggled with the marshmallow fondant trying to get it a more lush vivid purple velvet color, but very glad of the dough hook on my stand mixer, since I was able to multitask while it mixed the color into the fondant for me. I used the nose of a round piping tip to add tufted buttons to the chairs. When I was adding the fluffy fondant, I kept wishing I could sit down in one of those nice thick cushions!

The pipe organ was one of my favorite pieces I designed, so I'm very happy it turned out that well! I piped black chocolate over white marshmallow fondant for the keyboards, and the "carving" was the same brown royal icing as the rest of the furniture. The pipes are candy sticks royal iced to a gingerbread backing board and sprayed with silver luster dust, then the rest of the gingerbread front sits against the pipes glued to the wall.

## LAST LOOKS

You might have noticed in the original mockup that I had designed a mansard style L-shaped roof, but after several tries, it never held together due to the size and weight of the pieces, so it is not included in the template. Instead of that roof I used the woodplank frosting sheet scraps to cover the bare top foam core ceiling piece and set the top tower on that, which actually made the total height more manageable for viewing, and after I finished the Corpse Bride's full-length, handpainted, two-layered, tattered veil out of white fondant, she looked better on the lower level balcony than on top of the tower as originally planned.

Thankfully placing characters and decorating the yard went fairly quickly since those had been finished in advance and only needed to be set in place without needing any royal icing to anchor them. After I glued the Tasty Tombstones graveyard in place on the foil with royal icing and propped them up with cookie crumb dirt and chocolate rocks, I piped a dam of royal icing and set cookie crumbs into the dam all around the baseboard and the edges of the house, then I spooned cookie crumb dirt loose onto the foil-covered base, artistically sprinkling the chocolate candy rocks last.

However, that still wasn't all the final details! I had bought tiny bone shape candy sprinkles for window trim, so I melted more black chocolate then piped the window shapes on wax paper where I had traced the windows from the cardboard templates. I wasn't using my silicone mats since I discovered while unpeeling the piped chocolate railings that the mats don't bend easily enough. Wax paper works much much better, especially when you need to draw first to plan exact shapes. The chocolate set quickly, so I needed to heat an area with my butane candle lighter to place the rest of the bones. I made sure the chocolate was in the approximate shape, then after it set in shape but before it would shatter, I gently trimmed with a paring knife to get crisp clean edges. I'm really pleased with how these turned out as separate pieces, since piped directly over the house siding they would have been lumpy.

I made the door trim in separate pieces like the window trim which worked well. The chocolate starts melting in your hands of course, so I used more melted chocolate to pipe "glue" in place so they set firmly much more quickly than royal icing. It took a very gentle touch so I'm glad that only one window broke during assembly and it pieced together in place fine. It definitely made the house much more finished with all the trim in place!

The railings had to be placed last since I was worried about reaching over them, so I finished the shingles on the tower next. I had thought I would roll out thinner shingles, so I had melted

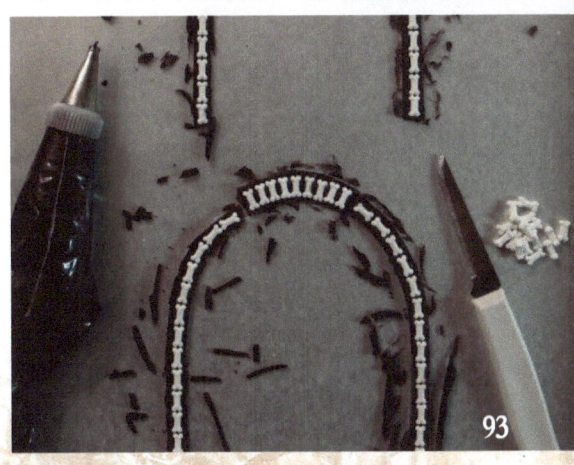

most of my candy discs, but since the bay window roof was already discs and I only had the tower left after giving up on the main roof, I just used the discs I had, including other colors when I ran out of black and painting with food coloring after they set. I had decided I didn't like the circle roof windows after all, so I shingled over them. Since I was already painting with black, I just painted all the roof seams without adding any extra seam trim.

I gave bonus points on the quiz for finding the denizens of Castle Brittahytta, including Miss Hermoine G Wells' and the Dark Duo, my black cats Ebony and Onyx. I sculpted both kitties from black chocolate, giving Onyx wider eyes and bigger fluffy tail hanging down from a comfy spot, and Ebony was in a classic windowsill pose with her skinnier tail curving nicely, just like she does.

It was finally time to pipe green royal icing spooky ivy all over the house and the gravestones. I liked the look that not as many leaves were growing but the scraggly vines had taken over for years. I covered the whole bay window and up to the main roof and around the front door, plus climbing the tree and all over the opposite side wall under the balcony. Even though the icing was too runny to hold the leaf tip shape, I think it still was effective. It sure was hard to mix a green that dark!

I am so relieved the web-pattern "wrought-iron" piped chocolate railings worked since they really improve the overall look! I had repaired the railing breakage from removing from the silicone mats, but I probably should have left them in sections since the long sections broke in multiple places anyway while setting in place. With so many railings around the main roof I decided the tower didn't need railings. I had piped the spiderweb brackets not knowing for sure where they would fit, but I absolutely love them on the tower!

I'm very glad the graveyard gate also survived assembly only glued to the foil on the baseboard! It nicely framed the graveyard pathway filled with more chocolate rocks. I had saved some cotton candy fog for the final photo shoot and took about 150 MORE photos once it was finally finished to my satisfaction!

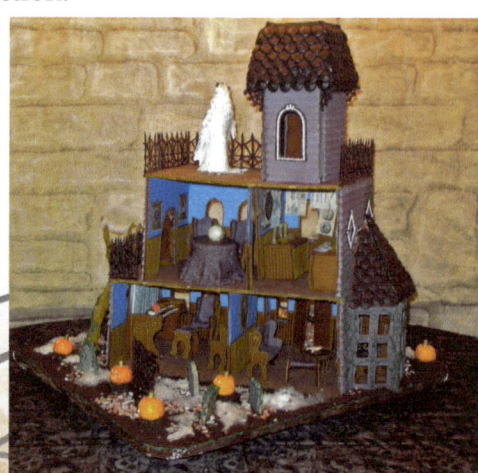

## GOING OUT IN A BLAZE OF GLORY

After spending over FIFTY hours creating the Ghoulish Gingerbread Haunted House for Halloween, where there was such a crowd leaning in to inspect the details that many people had to wait their turn for a closer look, I decided it would be really fun to keep it around for awhile and redecorate it for Christmas! After purchasing mini battery string lights and a bunch of quins in shapes of mini snowflakes, candy canes, gingerbread men, and assorted colors of edible pearls, I spent about another twenty hours in the redecoration project, until all the halls were decked with green royal icing, red & white starburst shutters were dripping with icicles, the laboratory transformed into Santa's workshop, the crystal ball was replaced by a mini gingerbread house, the Dark Duo's portraits appeared upstairs in place of the spooky Haunted Mansion spirits, lighted & decorated Christmas trees appeared inside and out, snowmen gleefully guarding the front and back, and sugar snow was everywhere, just in the nick of time for my annual Holiday Happy Hour party!

Then after Christmas was over, and the house was attacked further by curious kitties and started disintegrating, we decided it should go out in a blaze of glory!

Kids, do NOT try this without adult supervision! We are grownups, we had a hose at the ready, the grass was wet, the house was up on a firepit, and the fire was monitored the entire time until it burned out…and the moral of the story is that dry ice bombs can still go off 30 minutes late, so everyone stand back and be careful!

Since fireworks are illegal in my area, we used two small dry ice bombs plus flames burning about an hour afterwards to demolish it, until the only one left standing in the final flames was the backyard snowman!

## SPOT 13 SPOOKY STORIES ANSWERS

So, did you Spot all 13 Spooky Stories shown by the creepy clues & characters in & around the haunted house? Here are the answers!

1. Jack Skellington & Sally from The Nightmare Before Christmas were mischievously peeking out of the balcony windows

2. Emily the Corpse Bride was standing sadly up on roof on widow's walk

3. Dr Horrible's Sing-Along-Blog was represented by the Captain Hammer dartboard on the bulletin board in the lab

4. Edward Scissorhands sculpted the hand hedge in front yard

5. The Phantom of the Opera's face mask & red rose were on the pipe organ

6. The Picture of Dorian Gray was on the inside wall in the "attic" seance room

7. The Raven by Edgar Allen Poe "still is sitting" perched "above my chamber door" to the balcony

8. The Wizard of Oz 1939 film Wicked Witch of the East's legs in striped socks wearing the Ruby Slippers were sticking out from under the house

9. Madame Leota from Disneyland's Haunted Mansion was inside the color-changing sugar crystal ball, and two spooky Haunted Mansion portraits were in the seance room

10. Harry Potter's loyal owl Hedwig was holding a scroll perched in the bay window tree

11. The Addams Family's disembodied hand Thing was crawling on the coffeetable

12. Henry Jekyll's explanation letter and envelope to Dr. Utterson were on the table in Dr. Jekyll & Mr. Hyde's laboratory

13. Bill Compton's gravestone was in the graveyard for True Blood

Bonus characters the Denizens of Castle Brittahytta were a portrait of yours truly as Miss Hermione G. Wells behind couch, kitty Onyx on the lounge chair in the bay window, and kitty Ebony sitting in the front window behind the hand hedge.

Now not only do you know the full story of my giant Ghoulish Gingerbread Haunted House, but you can also go back and find any spooky stories you missed!

# Parting Words

I hope you enjoyed this helping of Halloween how-tos and will be inspired to adapt these ideas to host your own haunted happenings. If you ever find yourself so deep in party plans that stress starts overtaking the joy of creativity, stop, sit back, take a deep breath, and remember this: No matter how basic or elaborate you decide to be, above all the whole point is to have fun!

## Happy Haunting!

# Eerie Elegance Eats Extras

## SPOOKY SHOPPING

Here are some links to purchase some of the special equipment used in this book:

The Frightful Skull Fountain Kit, Original Artwork Antique Laboratory Labels and other eerie items are for sale at the Britta Blvd shop on Etsy:
http://www.etsy.com/shop/BrittaBlvd

Truffle candy molds perfect for Easier Eerie Eyeballs:
http://www.amazon.com/Wilton-Truffles-Candy-Mold/dp/B0000CFO6Y

If you'd like a spine model to go with your Violent Vertebrae:
http://www.amazon.com/Flexible-Desk-size-Vertebral-Column-Item/dp/B0009VLRJI
http://www.amazon.com/Lippincott-Williams-Wilkins-Chrome-Stand-SM91/dp/B000F10R66

Oven-safe silicone skull pans for Skones and Dia de los S'Muertos chocolate skulls:
http://www.amazon.com/Wilton-Scary-Skulls-Cavity-Silicone/dp/B0036Z9WTQ
http://www.candylandcrafts.com/halloweensiliconcookiepans.htm

Pumpkin Cookie Cutter Set with Cutouts used for the
Glowing Jack O' Lantern Cheese Ball:
http://www.amazon.com/OLantern-Cookie-Cutter-Assorted-Colors/dp/B001RUO7O2

All-black candy shell chocolate candies for Frankenstein Fingers:
http://www.amazon.com/Ms-Black-Milk-Chocolate-Candy/dp/B0080JI2L2
http://www.partycity.com/product/black+milk+chocolate+mms+7oz.do

Metal form to deep-fry Tasty Tarantula Spider Rosettes:
http://www.amazon.com/Kitchen-Supply-7101-Rosette-Spider/dp/B002D47IRY

Non-stick bone pan for Bone Breadsticks:
http://www.amazon.com/Wilton-Nonstick-Bone-Cookie-Pan/dp/B004W8VIRK

Non-stick life-size skull pan for Sourdough Skeleton:
http://www.amazon.com/Wilton-Dimensions-Nonstick-Skull-Pan/dp/B003XKZSDI

Smaller skull molds for Sinister Skulls Cream Cheese Calaveras:
http://www.amazon.com/Nordic-Ware-Haunted-Cakelet-Bronze/dp/B00Y6PRETK

Cookie stamps for Creative Calavera Cookies:
http://www.amazon.com/Fred-SPIRITS-Cookie-Cutter-Stampers/dp/B00B5EE1IM

You can cut your own gargoyle cookies using the template on the next page,
or purchase the same cookie cutter here:
http://www.amazon.com/Old-River-Road-Gargoyle-Cookie/dp/B00295QECC

Spiderweb cookie cutter for Ginger Web Cookies:
http://www.amazon.com/Ann-Clark-Spider-Cookie-Cutter/dp/B00KJ8I0P0

Spider cookie cutter for Fal-Awful Arachnids and Slimy Spiders:
http://www.amazon.com/Spider-Cookie-Cutter-Stainless-Steel/dp/B01GB3PF18

Silicone apple mold for ice apples in Bobbing Apple Punch:
http://www.amazon.com/gp/product/B00NZAA53E

Color-changing lighted ice cubes with non-replaceable batteries for Luminescent Laboratory Libations:
http://www.amazon.com/Litecubes-Brand-MultiColor-RAINBOW-Light/dp/B003YD9UGU

Submersible LED lights with replaceable batteries for Luminescent Laboratory Libations:
http://www.amazon.com/dp/B01C30NVDC

**TRICKS & TIPS**
Purchase Halloween clearance items for next year, and watch along the year since off-season prices might be on sale!

# GARGOYLE GUIDE

## Gingerbread Gargoyle Cookie Cutter Template

Trace this design onto thin cardboard & cut out,
place template on rolled cookie dough,
cut around template with a knife,
then pull away extra dough.

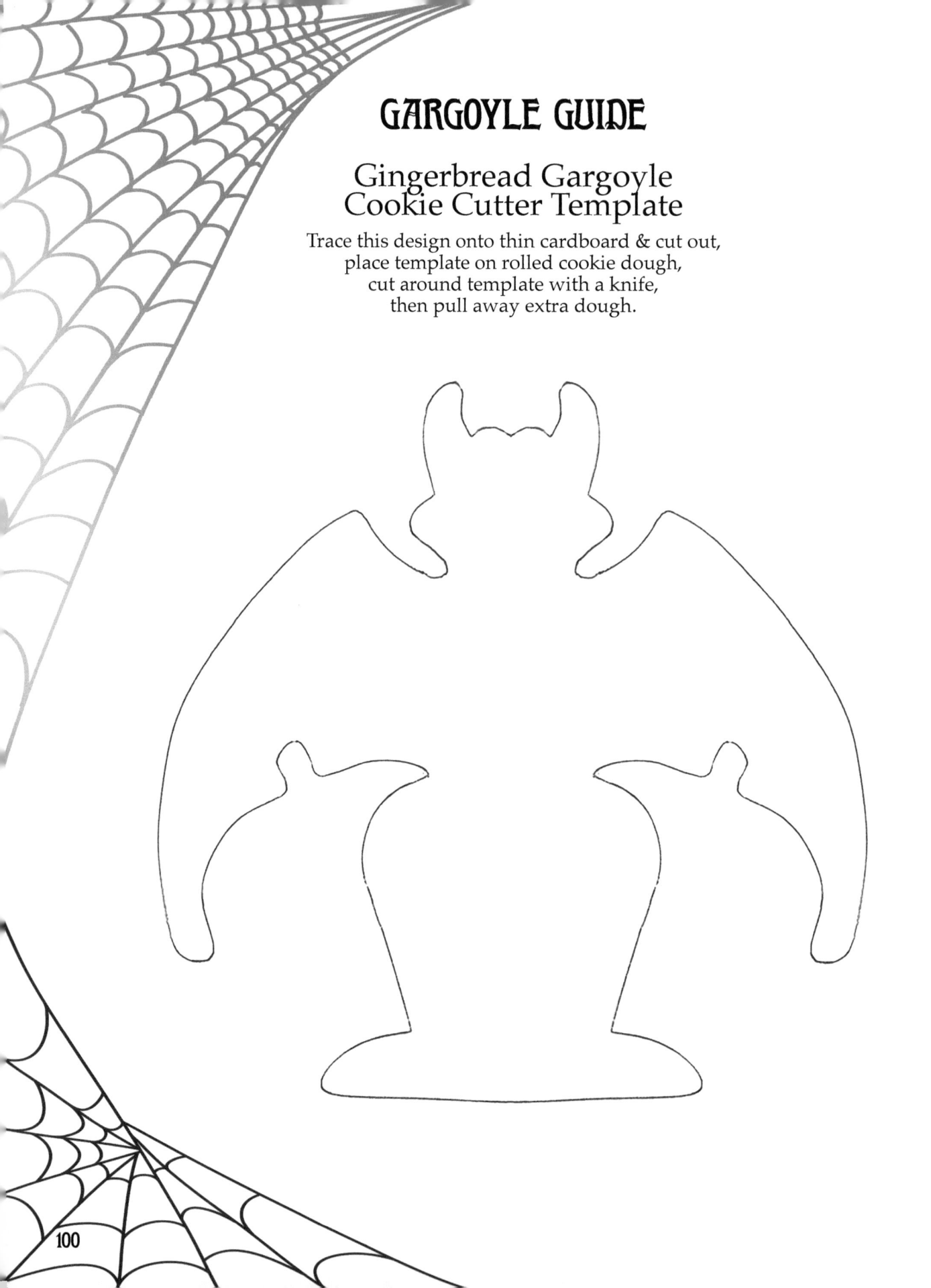

# CREEPY CUISINE CHEF CARDS

Copy these cards for your chefs to enter your Creepy Cuisine Contest.

## Britta Peterson

*Eerie Elegance Eats* is Britta's third book after 20 years of self-publishing her website Britta Blvd, where she is known as the "Webmistress of the Dark." Artistic and crafty from a young age, over the years she has turned holidays into opportunities for elaborate parties as performance art, transforming her home into an entirely new environment, especially for Halloween. Friends have called her "a cross between Martha Stewart and Tim Burton," which is a comparison she considers high praise. She currently lives in Santa Clara, California, with Ghoulish Glen and her two black cats, Ebony and Obsidian, who are too much of a handful to be in the same portrait with her!

www.ingramcontent.com/pod-product-compliance
Lightning Source LLC
Chambersburg PA
CBHW042008150426
43195CB00002B/55